R.O.N
Righteousness
Overpowers
Negligence
Volume 1

Ron Caldwell

Copyright © 2022 * Ron Caldwell

All rights reserved. No parts of this publication may be reproduced, scanned, or distributed in any printed or electronic format without permission.

Publisher: MzTU Fearless Writing & Publishing Services LLC.

ISBN: 9798841646129

DEDICATION

I dedicate this book to
my beautiful angel of a mom may she rest in heaven
Catha Jean Caldwell.

Thank you for always believing in my poetry.
the last thing you told me before you left this gracious
Earth was "boy go do something with your poetry".
Well, here it goes I hope you enjoy every word.

To all the young black men still trapped in this heartless
systematic oppressed world feeling like your hopeless
never give up.
Find your life's purpose,
we all have one.

CONTENTS

Dedication
Acknowledgments i

R.O.N part 1 Pg 3

R.O.N part 2 Pg 53

R.O.N part 3 Pg 96

R.O.N part 4 Pg 136

R.O.N part 5 Pg 182

About The Author Pg 237

ACKNOWLEDGMENTS

I gracefully would like to take the time to
thank a few people who mean the
world to me.

First off, praises to my spiritual being who shines his
reflection over me every time he enables me to see another
day here on this thing, we call
planet earth.

To all the people who believed in me and my writings
from the beginning,
you all know who you are.

To my brother from another mother
Leroy KT Thompson what is understood doesn't need to
be explained, thank you for always having my back since
the 80's until our present day.

Thank you for giving me the title
Priority Prescriptions and
Visions of A Visualizer.
You were the inspiration behind
P.O.P.S (Property, Oppressed, Persecuted, Slave)
R.I.P. Kenneth Thompson Sr.

To my cousin slash momma slash auntie
Cynthia McElroy
Thank you for everything you do for me,
you mean the world to me.

Thank you, cousin Bree
for the talks and
inspiring words when I'm feeling like
my anxiety is getting the best of me,

R.O.N

Thank you for the encouragement and
inspiring quotes
I love you for life.

To my only begotten son,
I know we see the world differently at times,
but you know that the world is yours,
so go capture it.
Go and catch your dreams and in
the meantime
don't let your integrity run away while
you're chasing your dreams.
I love you Ronnie Reality Caldwell
A.K.A SO3x.

Shout out to my brother Emmett Caldwell
keep being you and thank you for always looking out,
love you kid.

My brother Frederick Caldwell
you suffered a lot in 2020 but your spirit is still here.
Telling the people what you mean to me is a
whole other story.
You fought a good fight R.I.P.

To the mother of all mother's
this book will not be possible without your spirit over me.
We did it Ma,
I Love You.
Rest peacefully.

Thank you
Velverly Caldwell for being a big cousin, sister, and auntie
all balled up in one.
You are the mother of all mother's,
you and your outspoken daughter
Yachica (Twinkle)

R.O.N

You are amazing, Yachica.
Thank you for my poetry binder,
I put it to use.

To Uncle Fred I love you taught me a lot about myself as
an educated black man, thank you. OMAD 4 life!

To Iesha aka Bubblegum Caldwell, you saw my talent 20
years ago, thank you so much for typing out my poems
back in the day and believing in me.
I love you cuz.

And last but certainly not least,
to the teachers who criticized my stories,
except for a few who told me my stories were too long and
that by the time
I reached high school; I had a 5th grade reading level.
I dedicate this one to you as well.
Thank you!

To my publisher and my mentor,
Tasha Usher aka MzTU.
Thank you for believing in my vision.
You are a gift from up above.
I appreciate you, and
Thank you for publishing my art.

R.O.N

My Mom
Catha Jean Caldwell 1943-2014
& Brother Freddy Caldwell 1966-2021

R.O.N

CHAPTER 1

R.O.N

POEMS I

- **R**ighteousness **O**verpowers **N**egligence part 1
- How's Your Day Going?
- Black Lives Don't Matter
- Ghetto Misery
- Amerikkka Witta' Triple K
- A Letter 2 Amerikkka
- In A Perfect World
- B.U.L.L.E.T
  Before Unity Learn
  Life Eventually Turns
- Transparency
- A Slave In The Making

R.O.N
RIGHTEOUSNESS OVERPOWERS NEGLIGENCE
PART 1

R.O.N

Intro

Am I a demon or a Christian?
An atheist, or a Muslim?
Swarming through baptism.
Is there love or hatred?
Infidelity or greed?

Is blood thicker than water?
Am I a beloved seed?
My heartbeats tremendously
With poetry pen strikes,
Apocalyptic symptoms I use
When I write.

My generation is unaware.
Inferior to this social status.
The Armageddon is real it's not an
Impractical fabric.
I've got the blood of a master from a
Slave dripping from
My fingers. Plus,
My lines are mentally depraved.

Uncommon demeanors.

I hear by announce myself
The opposite of a clone.

All the rest of y'all will
Condemn to my throne.
It's catastrophic destruction
I'm ill with a pen.
Watch me euthanize y'all from
The form of a mercy killing.

R.O.N

Poison y'all animals for eating
The forbidden fruit.
We got caught up in an
Anti-movement not knowing
The truth.

Brainwashed through enslavement,
Even Jesus murderers
Thought he was
A spook.

Chased by the same
Killers who assassinated
Malcolm.

Righteousness
Overpowers
Negligence

Is the acronym of

R.O.N.

R.O.N

R.O.N

How's Your Day Going?
A Conversation with Revelation

Good morning,
How's your day going?

Mine is fine, can't complain.
Looking outside watching this movie
Trying to maintain.

How's your day going?

Mine is low-key.
Writing this script to the plague,
Trying not to get chased by the disease as
I cross the corner store to purchase
My cup of coffee.

How's your day going?

Mine is going by fast still
Isolated in an era of Trump.

How's your day going?

Mine is focusing on my next
Strategic move, as I
Roll this next one.

How's your day going?

I pray that your healthy.
With a mind that'll travel
Even without leaving home,
We can all become wealthy.

R.O.N

Wealthy of the mind though.
Blackman you're a star.
With a little bit of knowledge of
Self-trust.
We could go far.

How's your day going?

The sky is a mixture of
Blue and red.

Don't look too deep into it, just
Analyze what I said.

How's your day going?

Mine and yours could've been better.
But we chose to go
Our separate ways,
Instead of growing together.

How's your day going?

I apologize for asking the same thing.
But actually, thing's ain't looking
Bright under the sun,
Trying to dodge
Covid-19.

How's your day going?

My scriptures bled.
We are almost to our
Destination and his name
Shall be written on the servants'
Foreheads.

R.O.N

How's your day going son?
Well, here I am.

Looking at the
Earth move as the seals is opened by
The lamb.

How's your day going?

We gonna ride this one out together.
Look closely can you see
The climate change
There's a storm that awaits in
The weather.

R.E.M.
Rebels Ending a Massacre.

Losing my religion,
As well as my breath.
As the pale horse awaits and
His rider is death.
So, tell me.

How's your day going?

Mine is interrupted by
The last flood.
An inhabitant on
Earth with dirty blood.

Can you feel my heartbeat?
Can you see the vivid portrait of the stars?
From the sky falling to Earth,
As the figs drop from the trees.

R.O.N

Can you feel the infliction and
Destruction upon the earthquake?
The fire and hail that also awaits.

This is the making of the last kiss.
The sun that stood by
The moon that stood by
The stars that were darkened by
The abyss.

So, how's your day going?

Mine is fine.
I can't breathe with this mask on, but
I shall see you when the
World blows over and when
The four angels come back to
Kill a third of
Mankind.

Until then enjoy your day.

R.O.N

R.O.N

Black Lives Don't Matter

Righteousness
Overpowers
Negligence is the song I sing.

Steady chasing the paper money,

G.R.E.E.N.

God
Rules
Everything
Everywhere
Naturally.

Got my fist raised high
Embraced in black.

Political pollution, poverty.
We see all of that.
Where I'm at it's still corrupted,
We still living in shit.

Police destroying everybody but
Black lives get the short
End of the stick.
Over the fence it's a
War zone,
We still lost and imprisoned.

It's a cultural,
Social reconstruction until
We examine the obstacles and

R.O.N

Determine the vision.
By any means necessary.

Our whole life from
Birth is reviewed, no lie.
Up until the coffin is shut and
Our spiritual reflection meets us
Eye to eye.

Your death is written.
An older woman still catching the
Holy ghost as she shouts.

It's infiltration and
Trump want to keep
The Mexicans out.
Got the philosophy of
An angel on one shoulder
Protecting what's mine.

The other shoulder,
I felt atheism.

I was Satan a long time.
Evil don't care,
He comes in all forms.

Shooting up
Our homes in
Our country we've been warned.
It's hell downstairs,
Sniff the flames in the streets.

Illuminati captivated
666 marks of the beast.
Heaven and Hell.
The story of enslavement.

R.O.N

Money makes the world go round.
Jews and Mason's.
Facing my addiction in the
Mirror a man died with
A conviction,
A needle in his veins,
Gun in one hand, standing
Close to demons.

Them visions be tripping.
Then God interrupted,
Told me to get what's mine,
Now go and get it.

Black lives don't matter.
Black lives don't matter to
Anybody, even to us.

The truth we ignore.
Steady waiting for the
World to end as the spook sits by the door.

Black lives don't matter.

Black lives don't matter without
Knowledge of self.
Black lives don't matter
Because we don't love
Ourselves.

The negro constantly sells his
People out with a degree of
Non-intelligence.

The coon is dangerous,
The coon does it out of ignorance.
Ways of the d'evil,

R.O.N

Throw the rock
Hide your hand.
No weapons formed against
The righteous
Shall prosper to
Mentally break a man.

Get the righteous clean
Not by chains to bed.
Get the righteous clean by
breaking those mental chains,
Instilling knowledge in his head.

Had to clean my yard because
My grass was too high.
Cut off the head of
The rattle and watch
The snake
Die.

R.O.N

R.O.N

Ghetto Misery

DAMN,
The Lord's got a gun.
Momma's gone and
I lost a son.

I am,
The product of the crack epidemic.
Bathed in the hands of
Oliver and Reaganomics,
Nancy's my bitch.

I D.A.R.E. you to be a witness.

The FBI broke me in half,
Shattered my alliance,
Shot me with their poison
Animals that does the evil.
Became a victim of
The product of
The poison that destroyed
My community and the people.

Ghetto Misery,
I am the resurrection of the dark.
A Pisces
Political
Intelligence
Society
Crippling
Everything
Standing

A guppy's transformation into a shark.

R.O.N

These are the last days.
Basic
Instructions
Before
Leaving
Earth.

It's all logical.
We are standing in the
Puddle of the scriptures of
The last book of the
Bible.

Guerilla warfare,
When you sleep on
The floor you can't fall
Out of bed.

Guerilla warfare,
Times running out,
Time to paint these
Washington wall's red.
The ghetto is a jungle.

We are all critical and loose.
We are all prisoners of the mind
Who should be the gatekeepers of the zoo?

They called us
Little Black Sambo and Pickaninny.

It's miserable in the ghetto.
It's misery being stuck in the ghetto wounds,
Being taught by non-prophets.

Standing here a
Portrait of a depiction.

R.O.N

The lost lion,
A concealed object was only
Standing here fixing to march.
A lion turned into a
Black panther quick.

Free breakfast for the babies,
Buried in black leather
By the hands of the government.
A smooth and suave brother
In a chair, in a room,
In the middle,
Thinking of a master plan
With a pistol
With a shotgun in my hand
A portrait so memorable.

Ghetto Misery,
Now everything is so
Fucked up, a doomed child of confinement.
They could have never gotten
Us in shackles without
Our assistance.

Think about it.

Feeling like I lost
My sense of self.
In the ghetto where it's misery,
We need not stand alone in
Tribulations of a trial
We stand by ourselves.

Slept near the flowers in the attic.
Visions of falling,
You'll know the bottom
When you hit it.

R.O.N

Standing in the ghetto,
Drinking a corona
Inhaling the virus and
The symptoms that come
Along with it.

It's a national emergency,
Around the corner.
There's no new day,
Just the ghetto child
Who became a man,
Who infiltrated the C.I.A.

R.O.N

R.O.N

Amerikkka Witta' Triple K

I got a military army,
A million militants, army in the street, and
No man is smiling, this is

Amerikkka Witta Triple K.

Amerikkka witta triple k
In the middle of a warzone.

By any means necessary,
Death certificate,
Bury Amerikkka,
Cover him up with the
Amerikkkan flag.
Reads Uncle Sam on big toe.

I am,
The environment where life comes cheap.
Even cheaper when you're the product,
Sho' nuff'.

Found myself drowning by
D'evil's underneath
Black water.
I see my life span,
Underneath black water.

My good deeds and
Past memories,
Underneath black water.
Where reflection isn't eternal,
Underneath black water.
Where my goddess said

R.O.N

I am,
The reflection of a master to her
Underneath black water.

Where my infinite knowledge isn't
Inside of a fortune cookie,
Underneath black water.

Where momma said get up and
Engrave my writings to the world,
Underneath black water.

So, with the force of a glow over
My physical,
D'evil lifted my head
Underneath black water.

And he asked me
"Who am I?"

I answered back,
"God's reflection of a master",

I am,
The dragon of a last dying breed,
Against all odds,
Underneath black water.

Little black baby sitting in the
Middle of a white room,
Pamper on, raised in
Black dirt.

Born a sinner, ready to die, but
What's your death after
Your life when you're leaning up
Against that hearse.

R.O.N

Who wants to roll dice with your life?
You in the back, in black.

Feds can hear your conversation.
Solid structure like the firm,
Got your phone tapped.

Blood and white powder.
Blue chips and promises.

In the middle of a healing process,
The body is a wave of
Pure consciousness.

I am,
The same skin and knife
That punctured M.L.K..I.L.L
The death, lost, and
The dark.

Amerikkka has been
Dumb, blind, and
Incompetent from the start.
Hear no evil,
See no dark vision.

Perfect timing.
It's just the night of the comet,
Living dead turning into thriller,
Inside is black but with a
White outlining.
Clutching a tiger fist in the air,
A roaring lion kills.
No game.

Amerikkka eats the young.
What's the purpose of

R.O.N

Sharing those visions when
Your purpose has no gain.
A million and one soldiers with a
Military mindset.

Chess moves,
Strategically speaking is how you
Make progress.
Look into the lens,
The sequel of a real-life movie.

This is Martin at the Lorraine,
Malcolm at the Audubon,
Fred filled up with lead.
The assailant before entering
The room again to place another
Bullet in Hampton's head.

Heaven cried, fire
Making planets burst,
With every kiss of a tear
Set ablaze the Earth.
Cold summers and
Hot winters is over there.

Amerikkka is dying
Slowly and she's not playing fair!

R.O.N

R.O.N

A Letter 2 Amerikkka

Dear America,

The President doesn't care
For us blacks.
It's a political outburst an outcry
For us blacks.

America,
I'm almost ashamed to call this
My country.
The American flag went up in
Flames centuries ago.

We were slaves.
We still slaves.
It's a disappointment.

We are slaves as poets
Fighting for diamonds with blood on it.
Under the soil, the pavements
We hide yours.

The facts,
That's what we live for.
Over in Africa they die for.

In Sudan a mother sold
Her child off for twenty bucks,
To become a slave with
One meal a day.

Back at home we talk about
Bad luck.

R.O.N

Where in my country
We complain about the littlest things.
I'm also to blame.

A soldier wakes up
Praying today, it won't be his last.

While back at home
Donald Duck is still talking out his ass.

More cash is spent on war, that's
Reality, and
Flint still struggles for clean water.

Got my heart in tears.

While fake leaders are setting

Blacks back 100 years.
When will the cooning end?

Forget this,
I'm going to the Gucci store,
Right now.
I'm getting on this yacht,
Right now.
I'm dancing in front of these white folks,
Right now.
I'm sitting on this porch with a monkey,
Right now.
White folk still painting their faces black,
Right now.

Look at Christ
He stands at a distance.
We are standing at a distance
Through discipline.

R.O.N

Mom done gave birth to another
Crack baby, who cries in the
Dark, lonely, and hungry.

Yeah,
I could've wrote about
Ice and riches.
But this is my letter to
America, inhale this.

These artists egos goes
Above their work.
Making paper after their owners
Cuts his slice first.

This is my letter to America,
Even George W. Bush.
The same Bush behind
9/11, the button he pushed.
Sent my brothers overseas, stressed.

Forgot all about terrorist in
Iraq when there's
Terrorist in the U.S.

An American gets blown up in
Pakistan, now he's a hero.
While the exonerated five are
My heroes.

In my eyes there's
Hollywood lies, scandals, and drugs.
It burns inside of me the
Whole world is corrupt.

On a playground eating the
D'evils pie.

R.O.N

Looking through the lens of the
All-American lies.

Washed my hands in
Satan's mud, my body is unclean.
Fifteen years later
I'm still a product of New Orleans.

My lost body remains unquestioned.
As for the Government
This nation did nothing.

It hurts to see that the color of
My skin still matters in
This world full of sins.

My letter to America,
My cold body held on for a moment.
I can't find mommy.
My sisters dead body,
I'm still holding.
She was only three at the time.
She was dehydrated, too much for
A child so she lost
Her life.

In the mist of all of this.
The President came after the fact and
Did absolutely nothing.

It was like my city was a
Third world country.

We the people have lost
Damn near everything.

R.O.N

It'll never be the same,
No matter how much they try and rebuild.
The spirit is gone now,
As well as the will.

But where there is a will,
There is a way.
I'm trying to hold on for
God's sake.
But is it too late?

I was only sixteen.
This was my letter to America

Mr. President
Thanks for everything.

R.O.N

R.O.N

In A Perfect World

The rebirth, the calm before the storm.
Then the storm erupts the globe.
Warning us to stay awake, this is the end.

We deserve peace on Earth
We deserve acres but
We are being fooled by Presidential donkeys
Who kept hostage, the mule.

I dreamt I was anointed with
The blood of Nat Turner.

My great, great,
Great, great, great,
Grandmother was raped by
My great, great,
Great, great, great
Grandfather.

My soul is bothered.

I am honored to be the
Spirit of a tragedy.
The ancestral slave who was
Thrown in the Atlantic.
Feel the ocean breeze of the
Dark flesh that was slaughtered.
The flesh of my mother
Who turned blood into water?

I am a man trying to manage,
The golden apple that's still hanging,
Who finally fell but still standing.

R.O.N

I am a 39-year-old man
Dreaming of integration.
But died young before that
Dream was fulfilled holding on to
Complacent.

Triumphant visuals unification of a belief.
I was sold off at the auction,
A human being that became property.

My face dismembered,
Unrecognizable by
Satan's of the south.

The start of the civil rights movement,
A 14-year-old Chicago kid
Who never got a chance to live.
The experience of self-doubt.

They told me I'll
Never become nothing.
Hopes and dreams is not a must.

They said get your
Black ass out of that seat and
Go sit in the back of the bus.
They are sick of me causing
Trouble.

With your voice you're a threat.

Fifty-five years later
It's a conspiracy surrounding
My death.

Go march somewhere else.

R.O.N

Boy, get on your hands and knees.
They tried to destroy
My dignity, as the hounds bit me.

Shot me down cold in my
Own driveway as my children watched.
As I take my final breath
As my wife cry for this to
Stop.

60 years later
I was resurrected into
An intelligent Black man but
Still under attack.

I was shot in the head purposely in
My own vehicle
As my wife remained calm,
As my baby girl sat still,
Confused in the backseat.

I became the
First Black President with
The world on his shoulders
My hair structure went from
Black to gray in eight years.
Strong, but at times I felt weak.
For eight years, until I was
Replaced by the mark of the
Beast.

Do you know how it
Feels to be empty in a world that's
Against us?

Get out, there is too much distrust.
They put me in a holding cell

R.O.N

For 30 years still, no promises.

For the future,
I am still trying to be exonerated.

I've been here before,
I've been here from the start.
You can take my freedom, but you can't
Take a warriors' heart.

On the concrete,
I can't breathe.
Blood in my mouth,
His knee applied pressure to
My neck, as I call out to my
Deceased mother, who I'll be reunited
With soon as I take this last breath.

By the cause of Satan's children is
The reason it had to end.
By D'evil rituals who want
To make
Amerikkka White again.

What if I told you this was all made up?
That this is a scene through the
Lens of tell lie vision.

That everything I wrote is just
Hell being rewritten.
What if I told you every
Black man, woman, and child
Was still on their own land,
Holding each other's hands.

R.O.N

Peace on Earth was always here, and
That we all could see the
Beauty of the motherland.

What if I told you that,
The human race will judge you not by your
Character but the characters content.

What if I told you there was never
Such thing as a color?

Just a human seeing each other for
Who we be in a world of
Freedom of non-negligence.

Look over the sky,
Heaven is on Earth.
What if I told you we will live forever?
It sounds good,
In a
Perfect World.

R.O.N

R.O.N

B.U.L.L.E.T
(Before Unity Learn Life Eventually Turns)

Took the bullet from the
Barrel from my brother's gun
Shot him dead.
Looked in the mirror with visions of
Cane as I bled.

Put my sister on the corner made her turn tricks.
Fed her semen through a glass dick.

Took my hard-earned money from my taxes.
Invest in chemicals to die in Iraq.

End prostitution!
Why do we hurt our woman in the dark?

Took the last match from
Lil' Malcolm burned myself.
Life is hard.

Woke up in heaven and had a
Conversation with
Rosa Parks, on the back of the bus.
I pray, we are searching for a better way.
Searching for answers to
Unsolved mysteries looking for
Our prey.

Destruction, doormat,
Demonizing D'evil rituals,
The world is filled with
Rebels.

R.O.N

I burned with Aaliyah on her plane,
But brought home an angel.
So, when you see 22 doves in the sky.
That's 22 kisses.
22 cries.

Took my last ride with Left Eye.
Had an IV in my vein when I prevailed.

Did Christ take me?
Is it a spirit or a figment of an image?
Was there really Romans and nails?

Still, I'm just a poor and
Lonely boy whose considered a Nigger.
My body bleeds on Earth, but
My soul still floats in the
Tallahatchie River.

The bullet bleeds betrayal envy.
I was stuck with one last
Bullet that killed Nipsey.

What does our life mean?

They say there's only one way out of the hood.
Do you believe in one dream?
A King assassinated
One bullet struck on
One balcony.

Our life has a flatline, but is our life up?
Took the bullet from
John Lennon's gun.

R.O.N

Put it in another one, bring back a
Beatle aim his bullet at
Trump.
Snatch Marvin Gaye's
Bullet from his chest quick.

If John Lennon's
Bullet don't work,
Marvin's will silence the
President.

Leave Lincoln stinking next to
James Earl Ray, burn his corpse.

Martin suffered worse with
No remorse.

Revive Malcolm's body.
I hear 50 bells,
I hear 50 shells,
50 dead bodies rot,
50 smells,
Bring back Sean Bell.

The test of endurance.
Life is the gun and we are the
Bullets.

Don't be absent minded forever,
Don't let the sun burn.

R.O.N

It's a B.U.L.L.E.T.

Before
Unity
Learn
Life
Eventually
Turns.

Just some thoughts for the mind.
The flag burns in time.
Blood on white sheets,
Turned into blue we are still stars but
The unrighteous is
Blind.

R.O.N

R.O.N

Transparency

Control the narrative.

I am the light shining through this
Transparent object,
Composing through a hidden gem,
Through the intricate complexities.

Living in a robotic bubble,
Lucifers paradise.
Social media is nothing but a
Virus infecting our minds.
Leading us down a path of
Self-destruction D'evils destination, now
Life isn't complete.

L.I.F.E.
Living In a fucked-up Environment

Living seeing things for what it's worth.

Clearly life ain't sweet.

Transparency seeing through
The glass of desire.
Living to learn, growing through
The mistakes.

Your too intelligent to let your
Intelligence go to waste.

Life is fire, it burns.
Throw alcohol on that fire,
The flame is a wildfire as

R.O.N

The world turns.
These poems of freedom,
Ron this acronym is
Written on the wall.

The advocator of equality and then some.
The interpretation of
The writings of the redemption song.

It's the departure and
What summed up everything.
The message that was final, that
Stood for something.

I can see clearly now through
This glass, the product of a
Last project of a lost guinea pig.

The historically experimentation of an
African experiment.
Throat slit as an infant,
Mother didn't want me forced into
Slavery beloved.

Composing through the hidden gem, and
The light still shines through this
Transparent object.

R.O.N

R.O.N

A Slave
In The Making

You went from owning your land, once free
From being exiled and shipped through slavery.

Psychology uneducated.

The process of
Breaking and slave making.
Separation man, woman, and infants.
Breeding uncivilized children.
So, your offspring will be dependent.

You've been
Misguided, misinformed, and blind.

Human nature.
Keep the body but take the mind.
Break the will to resist.

History repeats,
Meaning it still exist.
Turn intellect into weakness quick.
Chains and whips.

When in submission the
African woman became a bitch!

Destroyed through the same principles
That we use in breaking a horse.
Destroyed the
Nigger man,
Nigger woman, and
Nigger boy.
Going in circles.

R.O.N

Revelations in the bible.
The world's spinning,
360 ways of a cycle.

Your no good economically.
So, you'll be forced with
Hard labor, with less pay.

Generation to generation
Torn apart.
Beat a nigger to the point of
Death.
Don't kill him, but put the fear of
God in his heart.
Now he's useless.

Pull the nigger woman from
The nigger man.
Train that bitch literally to eat from
Your hand.

It's designed this way, it's no other.

So, in the future you'll turn
Your backs on one another.

Reproduce a slave, genetically speaking.
Niggers are animals, and this is
The effect of cross breeding.
The future generation will be savages.

This pattern stays the
Same on my land.
Completion enslaves.
These illiterate fools.

R.O.N

Annihilate the uneducated youth,
Turn them backwards into
Ass backwards fuckin' mules!

Keep killing each other
Reload those bullets.

Put a gun in a nigger's hand and pull it.
It's all over niggers, soon as you blink.
Sooner or later your race will be extinct.

Brain still in chains,
Ignoring the truth remains, it's
Still the same.

For every nigger that dies
Another is born in vain,
To become a servant

So let us..... Make a slave.....!!!

CHAPTER 2

POEMS II

- **R**ighteousness
  Overpowers
  Negligence part 2
- They Killed Cornbread
- A Yo' My Man. It's The Hood
- Economical Warfare
- Kaffir Children
- Imagination (A Letter From Heaven)
- Isolation
- Institutionalized (Mental Healthcare)
- Dirty 30
- Karma

R.O.N
RIGHTEOUSNESS OVERPOWER NEGLIGENCE
PART 2

R.O.N

Thoughts From Reality

Thoughts from reality from
A young man's point of view.

Blood of Christ,
Shadow of Satan.
Blacks killing blacks' an eternal reflection.

Mind of Malcolm and Martin
Still wrapped in enslavement.
Money is power,
Evilness is the killer.
Diseases makes the world go around.

Genesis is done with, revelations deeper.

The devil gave birth to me.
God tried to raise me, strangled.
Left me to be raised by animals.

Church lies &
World scandals.
War eruptions,
Wildfires,
Homosexuality.

Sodom and Gomorrah,
Woman dressed as men,
Men dressed as woman.
Burning in the flames, we dead already.

Still, I remain calm.
Write my life visioning reflections of
Myself through an
Eternal mirror of
Self-hatred.

R.O.N

Holding my breath,
Anxiety got my heart racing.
My son is one step through
Adolescence and I'm pacing.

Still praying.

Got righteousness wings on one shoulder,
The other there goes neglection.
Righteousness over stands
Neglection, still defiance is present.
Heaven can wait!
Smell the poverty in this dark room.

Came up in an era of gunshots,
G-boys, Black Mob,
Legion of Doom.
A loose cannon.

This pill is calming my nerves.
If these walls could talk, well,
They're talking just observe.

A prisoner to pain,
Recovering my life.

Zimmerman shouldn't be free.
My mother told me to
Wear my hoodie
With pride.

Haunted memories 2020 visioning,
Do you see the destruction?

It's underneath our noses,
Take a sniff of the cocaine
It'll bust you open.

R.O.N

This is my introduction,
God speaks,
Satan with a chip spoke as well.

I'm more than a dreamer but
A thinker,
A poetical revolt leader,
A king amongst kings stuck in the 90's
A rebel.

Today is deleted,
Tomorrow is an illusion.

R.I.P.

Trayvon, E. Gardner,
Freddy Grey, and
Ms. Bland.

Until we all meet, we are forever your students.

Rest in peace!

R.O.N

R.O.N

They Killed Cornbread

Cop shot a kid.

Cop shot a kid, look at him bleed.
Cop shot a kid, look at him bleed,
In the middle of the street.

Cop shot a kid!

That kid was me.
On my way home
I can still hear the sounds of
The raindrops knocking
The concrete.

Trey still holding his
Skittles and iced tea.
The basketball bounced so
Rhythmically in my
Own zone.
So, I never heard the sound of the police.

In the ghetto the skies are grey and
The black clouds that
Followed Nas,
Follows us all, each and every day.

The world is ours, but we are
Still bleeding constantly not breathing.

As cops killed me,
Gunned downed for no reason.
Time to paralyze this country.
We shouldn't have to live in fear.
We should police our own communities,
Liberation is near.

R.O.N

I'm running, running trying to
Beat these streetlights.

I'm running to catch curfew, plus
Mom is frying chicken tonight.

I can still hear the frantic
Screams of the neighborhood,
Echoing in my head.
As the community yells

"They killed cornbread"!!

"They killed cornbread"!!

Was it mistaken identity?
Was it just policemen not having anything else to do?
Was it hatred that lies from within?
Was it just the pigment complexion of my skin?

Yep, all of the above.

Using me as the identity that was
Mistaken for a cover up.

"They killed cornbread",

Mommas only child,
Laying on the ground,
Another future gone to waste.
Freddy is looking up at the
Sky that's still grey.

"They killed cornbread."

Could've been the next
Kobe but now

R.O.N

I'm gone.

While Mike Brown watched
On the sidelines,
He still had his
Headphones on.

My main man Alton Sterling
Was selling his music when
It happened.

While Sandra was in a police car
Ten feet away when this tragedy happened.

Emmett smelled death in the air,
He felt the trouble.
He shook his head sadly,
Can still see the sadness as
He looked puzzled.

Momma looked out of the window,
She sensed in the air the violence.
As the commotion grew louder,
She went in silence.
She panicked, felt her child was in
Danger around her.
She felt the spirit of a ghost during this
Crazy scenery.

As she ran closer,
She could see her baby's body
Lying dead, stiff in the street.
Police couldn't hold her
Back for too long.

"They killed my baby",

R.O.N

They killed **our** babies.
Mothers, please stay strong.

They killed our babies, but
With cornbread they picked a winner.

It's sad, there are more
Cornbread's that'll get
Gunned down and won't make it
Home for
Dinner.

R.O.N

R.O.N

A Yo' My Man….
It's The Hood…

8:37 a.m.
The sun has risen on the east.

Monday starting off
My daily activities,
Green tea, with a pinch of
French vanilla, before
I run these angry streets.

Thank you, Lord, for another day.

It awaits my way.
Staring at the bright clouds,
Thinking of life in the future and
How some survived 2020.

Well today was a good day,
Ice cube chills my
Poland spring.
Gazing into the eyes of the
Old lady on the corner as
She sings a melodic tune I've never heard before.

Wondering how she became of this.
Where did her life go wrong?

As she remains on the corner
Concentrating on her task,
As she twirls a skinny stick.
Glass bottles broken; little girl dressed more
Provocative than her own momma.
Weed dealer grabs her wrist,
Causing infuriating drama to come.

R.O.N

The future has looked us dead
In the eyes, literally.

R.P.D. passes by ignoring
The mayhem,
The chaos,
The confusion,
The madness,
The pandemonium,
The tumult in
The streets.
The breeze
Turned into smoke.

Arabs own our neighborhoods
On every corner.
Can't get upset with them though.
We are the ones who dropped
The ball.
Searching for help.
Crying for acres, and what should be ours.
Searching for ways to connect
The dots through generational wealth.

Love what my son is gaining,
He has his own merch.
A plan he's trying to master.

While we embedded
Cold hearted dreams, and
Billion-dollar visions, but awake to
Disaster.

Cataclysm not a trial of conviction.
A meltdown in these streets,
Nineteen and with a life sentence.

R.O.N

A lot of upheaval
Disruptions waiting for
The hourglass to stop,
The little provocative girl who was
The victim of being antagonized by
The weed dealer,
Then went and got her cousin.
Young kid, who raises himself,

Life is about to end.
The result of choices.

The nineteen-year-old
Who managed to get a life sentence,
Then went and shot the dealer
Who grabbed the little girl's wrist.

Garbage bags ripped open,
The smell of the funk heats up
The concrete good.
Garbage man just leaves it there.

I yelled,
Are you gonna' pick this mess up or what??!!

He hollered back.

A yo' my man!!

It's the hood!

R.O.N

R.O.N

Economical Warfare
(Big Business)

Savages and demons' destructs
The face of the earth.
So called Angels and Priests
Capitalize on life's living for what it's worth.

As long as eternity smells
Like death has risen from
The grounds of dead souls.
There will be puddles of blood to go around,
Immortal pain,
Breathtaking stress, and
Frustration that'll unfold.
As the eternal smoke is gone with the wind.

Waving anger cannot cope with the
Inner city living, the inner-city blues.
The inner-city catastrophe
That is so bruised up.
White sheets remain heartless
Hiding in blue fog.

Police brutality became hatred amongst us all.
We crawl, scrambling for
The American Dream.
We are Africa's hidden gem,
A diamond that still gleams,
Persecuted for what we believe.

In my heart there's a covering pattern,
I am losing oxygen as
I stand on holy ground.
My temple lost faith as
I came tumbling down.
I picked myself up

R.O.N

Reconstructed from the grave.
Still spitting on critical concrete
Surviving minimum wage.

Economical warfare,
Prisons flood with innocent children
Turned out by red flesh.

They became victims,
Shattering their own mirror, too much
Stress to digest.

So, we stay being called
Savages and demons,
Nothing more than
Drug dealers and crack abusers.
Alcoholics and cocaine users.

That's us endangered beast
Sniffing for our prey to eat.
Until we fill up all the cages and
When we are all deceased.

Savages and demons,
New World Order is about
The centralization of power.

Illuminati the enlightening one's
The American dollar.
The days of the red hat is in pursuit.

White America,
Thank you for inviting me to your home,
The land of the cheap prostitute.

Ghandi's lack of knowledge,
Innocence to his ignorance.

R.O.N

A King's hero,
History is concealed, and
War is big business.

A King lives on a throne.
Soon as the King entered the crisis of economy, that
King was dethroned.

We are the leaders of
Unnecessary spending always
Purchasing stuff we don't need from
People who hate us.
To impress people
We don't even know.

Green images, old slave owners
That's racist, like we got
Money to blow.

There are levels to this,
My poetry is my investment.
Standing on top of a pyramid
With one eye open controlling the
World like free masons.

It's that deep.

R.O.N

R.O.N

Kaffir Children

We are the world in a
Galaxy of anxiety of
Self-doubt, clinging on for
Self-hope.

We are the lost children, the lost race in
America hanging on for dear life in a
Corner of a box of
A Plato, so demented.

We are the hungry children,
Hunger for hope.
Placed here, forced with religion and no goals.

We are the descendants of ignorance
Afraid of success.
Stressed because of the
Pressures put in front of us.

We bleed insanity,
A glass easily broken.

We are the disloyal,
Incompetent, mind breeding betrayal.
The kids of Israel,
The unsatisfied children.
We are the scarred children
Basing everything off luxury.

But me personally,
I'd rather have one dollar to my name
Than one million,
If it means, I have to compromise
My integrity.

R.O.N

Everyday I'm trying to be a better me.
I was a hero to my child but am I still
That same hero?

We are the children that can't manage,
The children of a lost generation.

Look at me as a hero, and
A hero ain't nothing but a sandwich.

We are the descendants of
Ignorance, an offspring of
Nigger children.

That's what we call ourselves today.
So, don't get angry when they
Look at us as
The Kaffir child.

The **nigger** seed who did not get away.

R.O.N

R.O.N

Imagination
A Letter From Heaven

I see you never miss my birthday,
I reached out caught a
Blue balloon above the clouds,
Felt the drums sacred rhythms.

When it rains it's me,
Crying laughter, so by
The bronze grave maybe my spirit
You'll feel it.

Man, you've grown into a soldier
6 foot 7 by far.

That's because our spiritual being wanted
Your growth to make it
Easier to reach for a star.

Imagine heaven on Earth and
Everything was an illusion,
Pretty much a bad dream.

The dreams you have when
You're on Earth, when
You're asleep is pretty much
The actual thing.

In other words,
Love it while it last because it's
Only an image son.
See it for what it's worth, at least try.
Because living, really begins
When we all die.

R.O.N

It's a beautiful thing, glory.
Keep writing, sometimes people
Need to hear your story.
Instead of assuming they know your story.
Stay out of those cages,
They can't keep our minds locked forever
Captive in jail.

Watch who's watching you son,
When the loyalties gone the
Truth shall prevail.

I felt like the majority of people
Who was supposed to be family was
Fake as Hell.

That's why on Earth
I was secluded alone by myself.
Oh well, can't dwell on things
That don't exist now, son.
Focus on the future.

I'm living in the present.

In the afterlife don't want to steer
You in the wrong direction, and
Block my blessings.

Keep rising to the top.
Keep pursuing your music.
Don't compromise for a quick buck.

Remember they love our culture but
Hate our guts but hate
They ain't us.

R.O.N

Remember I'm here.
I ain't going know where, but
The place y'all call life has its doubts.

You'll grow old though.

I apologize,
I never got a chance to meet you son.
Sometimes when you're in pain
Death seems like a better way out.

Now I'm living.

R.O.N

R.O.N

Isolation

I live in my head
Steady spinning can't
Keep this head high.
Incognito writing away the
Discussions of my life.

I live in my head
Searching for a better way,
In depth with the
Complex conclusions you
Could never understand or
Even figure me out.

I live in my head but the tears
Spills from my mouth.

I live in my head
Asleep through memories
Feeling the fire blare.

We ignore our dreams too much to
Focus on nightmares.

I live in my head
Isolated through isolation.
Erasing pain defining the
Past studying the
Present of my presence.

A gift with a glow,
A golden child living with
An honor.

Mom gave birth to me but
I was raised by the father.

R.O.N

This is the curse that became a gift.
The attention span is only 5 seconds.
It ain't what you know, it's who you're in
The room with.

What's going on?
I'm outside but I know
The rules of a
Criminal.

I live in my head,
Not a victim of street
Circumstance but a
Hood individual.

My demise is on hold
Feel the endurance of
The purple rain.
Ice in my pen circulating
The heroin in
My veins.

Didn't understand death
When my best friend was
In peace as she rest.

Only 3 thought she was
On vacation, and she'll be
Back home in a sec.

People who came in my life
Usually came and went,
Nothing is permanent,
Nothing last forever,
Everything seems to be
Made up,
Abnormal,

R.O.N

A disguise,
A trace.

Everything is rotting while
We wear a mask
Over our face.
We are born to live
Only to die.

Seen children raped and
Kidnapped in front of
My eyes.

Mommy lived in the same
Household but unaware of
What's really going on.

Isolated to the fact that
What I thought was normal
Was really
Wrong.

R.O.N

R.O.N

Institutionalized
(Mental Healthcare)

My mother just passed
From a stroke.

My father passed
He had a drug addiction
He was strung out on
Dope.

My sister is on welfare,
Dreams she's chasing.
Her son was born suffering
From retardation.
He's a sickly child as well as all of us.
He has a case of chronic asthma.
Plus,
She's pregnant as we speak.
To bring another child into
This world, she could barely feed.

My homey Pop's is a
Vietnam vet.
Nearly lost his life living
Check to check.
The youth call him
Crazy.

Absent minded
Because of the things he's
Been through in the 70's.

Returned home,
Mentally wounded, in God we trust.

R.O.N

He drinks the pain away,
Slowly dying.
Decades of deadly chemicals
Mixed in his blood.

Who will help us?

Some of the brightest people
Suffer from mental health issues,
But feel they have no hope.
So, they
Slide down a slippery slope,
With no place to go.

Damn I'm confused,
My momma's dead, and now
I'm suffering from
Mental health issues.

Does anybody care?

My uncle was a boxer.
Hit one too many times
Causing brain trauma.

No insurance to see a decent doctor.
So, he's depressed,
Isolated living
Low-key.

Depression with suicidal thoughts,
Broke and lonely.

They're killing our babies with
The injections, infants from birth
Infected with the capsules and needles.
Poison they give the infants.

R.O.N

The children are
Dying, brain dead, becoming autistic.

Mental healthcare,
Meaning they need more facilities for
The people who suffer from
Mental health.

Instead of pills,
Infections is in us.
We need help!

To get us the proper understanding of
This condition.

Just don't put us in a
Mental ward.
Give us the proper education.

Your past can affect
Your future,
Physically, and
Mentally.

They do it with the medicine.
They do it with the food.
They do it psychologically to
Keep us in a bubble.

If Kevin would have gotten
Help before his
Mental got worse.

If it would have been
The proper healthcare,
The proper institute for him,
Maybe we could have gotten him

R.O.N

The help he needed.
Before he shot up those people in
That church.

I am the voice of
The voiceless of
The people, a mental health thing.

This isn't a black or white thing,
This is a disease thing, a mental healthcare
Thing.

And once again,
Give us the proper education that
We all need.

R.O.N

R.O.N

Dirty 30

Met Mrs. *P*
A few years ago.
Afraid of her at first
Because she was
So powerful.

Only 30 years of age but
She's been around the corner
A time or two.

White woman, small for
Her age and size.
Introduced by a family member
Eventually she severed our ties.

Wanted to marry
Mrs. *P.* myself I thought
She'd be the love of
My life.

Had me thinking about
Her days on end,
Kept me up all night.

Our first kiss was
Inexpressible, had me in
The wind breathing for
Her taste and feel.

In cabs stalking her down in the
Rain,
Sleet, and
Snow.
She's, my baby.

R.O.N

My dirty 30.
A freak in and out of
The sheets,
Can't resist her,
Can't let her go.

Use to party with her friends,
We'll all be up for days.
That's what the hours
Turned into.

Couldn't stand when
She left me lonely,
Had me stressed, even
Had me in the hospital.

But that didn't matter because
She followed me,
My baby had me.
High and dazed.
But always left the hospital
Feeling amazed.

Mrs. *P* was still in my heart
Even though I knew this feeling
Would not last.
Even though
Mrs. *P* was taking the
Majority of my cash.

I'm tired of you,
I want you out of
My life.

Don't want you as
My dependent for the

R.O.N

Rest of my life.
Plus, she became
Violent and rude.
Couldn't stomach her any longer.

Mrs. P had me
Throwing up my food.

Addicted to Mrs. P.
Even though
She was bad luck.
She got so violent
She'd scratch my legs and arms,
Leaving them bloodied all up.

It's time to leave Mrs. P before
She ends my life, but
Her sex is so
Addictive.

I can't pretend.

It's time to give her
Back to my cousin who introduced
Me to her.

That was three years ago and
I haven't looked back at
Mrs. Percocet 30 milligrams,
Ever since.

YOU CAN HAVE THAT *BITCH*!!

I'M DONE!!

THE END!!!

R.O.N

R.O.N

Karma

The energy you put out into
The universe is
The same movements you'll get back lessons,
Well learned.

Not knowing the controller controls
Every single thing we do.

It will come back holding
More weight on this planet
We call Earth.

Debra was an abusive mother
To her only child.
Lord knows that child tried.

One too many hits left
The child with years of
Psychological pain, until
Debra's only child died.

Fast forward,
Debra was never charged for
Her only child death.

Fast forward years of
Frustration and regrets, up until
Debra took her last breath.
Debra died a horrible death,
With cancer that was in her breast.

That only got worse and eventually spread,
Plus, Debra suffered badly.
Ten times worse than

R.O.N

Her only child did.
Cancer was the cousin, but
Karma was the energy that
Came and did the job
Really quick.

That being said, we all have some
Karma we all must face.
Whether it's good or bad.
Karma could be critical to
The human race.

Words to live by questions unanswered.
Who are we to question **karma**?
Who are we to trust in your God?
Who are we to believe in your religion?
Who are you to define our history?
In a time when times are hard.
We were created on
Purpose with a purpose.

As the warm wind blew.
Tough times never last, but
Tough people do.

Karma bites with venom from
Different angles, you'll never
Know when
She'll come and visit you.
This thing called
Karma.

R.O.N

CHAPTER 3

POEMS III

- **R**ighteousness
  Overpowers
  Negligence part 3 (The Reason)
- Pleasure
- Angel In A Scorned Dress
- Coolie High
- Coming To America part 1
- If Bishop Was Alive
- What Would Nip Do?
- H.E.R.O
  (Hoping Everything Reaches Out)
- A Poem 4 Cat (Catha Jean Caldwell)
- A.N.X.I.E.T.Y
  (Another Night X Illusions Ending Thoughts of Yesterday)

R.O.N
RIGHTEOUSNESS OVERPOWER NEGLIGENCE
PART 3

R.O.N

The Reason

Living in the sun
Through the son
I'm formally, mentally baptized
With wisdom,
Soulful knowledge is precise.
Aborted in the cold that's too
Real to be right.

I write,
For the uneducated who wasn't
Blessed with the ability to
Become doctors and lawyers.

I write,
For the victims on the east,
In the middle our soldiers.

I write,
For all the children
Caught up in life's turmoil.

I write,
For the babies
Still dirty under the soil.

I write,
For the fathers who don't want to
Self-destruct, trying to sustain.
The fathers that'll do anything for a family.
I am trying to break that chain.

R.O.N

I write,
For the single mothers
Raising kids alone.
My black girls lost in one home.

I write,
For the black men still
Trapped in the system.
Surviving in this cold world
Still trembling.

I write,
For our forefathers
Assassinated, shot up for a cause.
Malcolm, Martin, Lumumba
We salute you all.

I write,
For a failed system and betrayal.
A hard blow I was
Hit with.

I write,
For you all still walking the streets
Acting like karma don't exist.

I write,
For all the revolutionist in
This modern-day.

I write,
For my adversaries for them
I pray.

R.O.N

R.O.N

Pleasure

Meet my sister Pleasure,
Isn't she lovely?
A beautiful butterfly in
The wind.

Pleasure isn't my blood sis,
We might as well be
Biological sisters.
Pleasure is my best friend.

Many people say we could be
Twins.
Same size,
Same height,
Same complexion.
Identical dimples on our right cheeks.
She's, my homie.
Laughter we shared
Since we were eleven.

As the world turns.

Pleasure became
Empty, lost, sad, and
Depressed inside.
Her warm empty heart became really cold.

It was like an angel came from
The heavens and took away
Pleasure's soul.

Throughout the years
Me and Pleasure
We took separate paths in life.
I became a doctor in

R.O.N

The field of anesthesia.
Pleasure became a stripper, a night drifter.
Walking the dark streets at night.

May God be the judgement.

Pleasure will always be my girl.
Had dreams of escaping
The dark nights, that may never
Turn into day.

She dreamed of traveling the world.

Pleasure wasn't always a
Delightful fulfillment.

Pleasure was once filled with pain,
Not in the literal sense, but
Through the agony of
Feeling defeated.
The pain of affliction.
The suffering this woman had to
Endure since Pleasure was a baby.

Mother died when she was
Only three.
Raised by her grandmother,
A five foot even
Little dark-skinned lady.

But even Big Momma
Passed away when
Pleasure was in her pre-teens.
The adolescence stage.

No father who loved her.
Pleasure was a runaway,

R.O.N

Knee deep in the streets.
She met Derick,
A slim young man, who showed
Pleasure love.

Well, something she felt was love,
A type of feeling you can't
Cover up.

He started off typical,
Whispering sweet nothings into the ear of
Pleasure as she falls into a
Spell we didn't see coming.

Derick had us all fooled.
Derick also suffers from pain,
Dealing with his own mental health issues.
His own insecurities,
Derick was the jealous type.
He said he'll never hurt
Pleasure.
Before he sees her in more pain
He'd rather take his own life.

Derick never got help for his
Own pain he endured.
Derick died young,
Suicide and it hurts me inside.

I think about this hurtful
Situation often.

Meet my sister Pleasure,
Isn't she lovely?
A beautiful butterfly in
The wind.

R.O.N

Touching my sister's
Cold dimple as
She finally looks peacefully.

Sleep in her own coffin.

Rest In Peace Pleasure.

R.O.N

R.O.N

Angel In A Scorned Dress

Can you hear my cry against the window pain?

Shattering glass crushed the
Walls of my soul.
Gone too soon over the black moon.

Can you see my shadow?

The spirit, the angel of a ghost.
Confused with my sexuality
No one can hear my careless
Whisper in the dark.

I cover the stains before
I departed the ocean.
Heaven's water covers my flesh.

I lived a quiet life but
Suffered an enormous death.

The beatings of my heart
Spills with the logic of acceptance.
I just wanted to be looked upon as
A normal young lady.
But my head is spinning at a great amount,
A high rate, tremendously.

How can I hold this secret?
The secret lies from within.
How can I hold this?
In an era where the young isn't
Blind to the fact?

R.O.N

My family along with mommy turned on
Me.
Mommy turned her back.

It's hard being a gay woman,
Let alone being
Black.

Oh well what's done is done.

I apologize for the pain I caused.
I don't deserve to live so, my favor to you
I will end it all.

How did you all not know?

My room been dirty, since
I was a child.
Skeletons in the closet dwell.

I'm better off gone!
My apologies to you
Mommy for taking the easy way out.
I can't take no more.

Sorry.
I couldn't live to tell
Mommy.
I was scorned for life.

R.O.N

R.O.N

Coolie High

I want to live forever!

That was the writings on the wall,
I want to explore the
Heaven's hill exploring
The concrete jungle,
Here on this
Planet Earth.

I want to live forever!

A proud young black child
Embracing the wounds of his adolescence,
Punctured the walls of men.
I'm a perfect picture a pure testament.

I want to live forever!

In peace, a peaceful journey writing about
The ghetto life as the days turn.
Laughing looking at the
Hourglass as time passes the young.

I want to live forever!

Roaming the hallways in school not
Looking at the ways of the future,
How I developed, and
How it all begun.

I want to live forever!

A bastard child,
Poppa was a stone rolling down a high hill.
Mountain top.

R.O.N

I just want to be me,
Dream until I am free, and
Erase the darkness of the minds that are
Blocked.

I want to live forever!

Sipping wine in a circle with friends.
Pouring out a little for
The brothers who ain't here.

As the preacher preach begins.
The teacher asked me,
"What do I want out of life?"
Had to think as I had to say.

I want to live forever!

Cause it's so hard to say
Goodbye to yesterday.

R.O.N

R.O.N

Coming To America
Part 1

Aye can you see,
I'm coming to America.

Can't wait until my flight touch down,
My family has been in your country for
Probably about five years.
Could not wait to join
My father, brother, and sister.

Life in America.
Did I choose?
Or did this beautiful country choose me?

America, America, America!!
What a blessing and a great place to be.

My brother facetimes me every day.
Showing me places to go and places to eat.
Things to analyze.
Books to read and what to study.

Allahu Akbar all praises due to the
Most High, guide me with your blessings.
Protect me and my loved ones.
Merciless one as you shield me with
Your spiritual presence.

Glorious it will be,
Escaping the atrocities of
The past killed in
Yemen.

R.O.N

War is still a part of a vision because of
A decrease in famine.
The epidemic of malnutrition was
Increasing a drastic mortality.

I love my people, but
I'm so tired of the water scarcity.

So, in 2015
I had no choice but to leave.
My proud Poppa is the owner of
Plenty businesses on
Plenty of urban street corners.

I have arrived to join them.

Kissed my father, brother, and sister
Looking around this freedom of living.
Met some unusual individuals with
Stories of being caught up in the system.
But doesn't realize that knowledge is
Infinite to them.

Fast forward.

Been in America for only 18 months.
Proud Poppa could not be more
Proud he fulfilled his dreams.

Myself, my older brother, and baby sister are
Here in the United States.
A well put team.

But for every good thing,
I never thought
I would do a drastic 360.

R.O.N

In one of our family stores
There was a situation of an
Armed robbery.
It was a Thursday night.

Two teens with
Black hoodies entered
Approximately around 11:55 p.m.,
5 minutes before midnight.

Proud Poppa was closing early,
They entered in and demanded
All the money out of the register.
Guns were drawn on Proud Poppa.

It all happened so fast.

11:55 p.m.

Myself and my cousin was putting the
Money in the back.
When in the front looking at the
Cameras, Poppa was
Under attack!!!

What shall we do Allah!? Help us!
As me and my cousin are in a state of shock.

Poppa panicked,
Made a sudden move as one of the two teens
Let off a firing shot. Bang!
The teens panicked and made a
Run for the entrance.

While Poppa lay in a pool of blood

R.O.N

With a gunshot wound to the chest.

Proud Poppa fought hard to
Escape the country of
Yemen.

Dead at 52!

By the same young unusual individuals.
I spoke about earlier.
With stories of being
Caught up in the system.

Now Poppa who died Proud
With integrity, died attempting to save
What he worked hard for in a
Country that also deal's with mass hysteria.

He is deceased now reunited with his wife.
Dead at 52!

Coming to America.

R.O.N

R.O.N

If Bishop Was Alive

Twenty-eight years ago
I was accidentally killed.

Or was it really an accident?

Twenty-eight years ago,
From my best friend.

Let's go back, I mean way back.
Baggie jeans, hoodies,
Carhart's and Timbs'.

Twenty-eight years ago,
Seems like a lifetime ago
Me and my brothers ran
Wrecking crew, nonstop.

Until my ego and pride got in
The way of brotherhood and this thing,
We called respect
(JUICE) got me killed.
Twenty-eight years ago,
Off that rooftop.

Wanted to be the leader.
The bad guy,
My mental state was on the line.
I was sick.

Wasn't no one man above the crew,
You know that shit.

Damn ain't no telling
Where I could be.
Where I would be if I was alive.

R.O.N

Maybe a testament to
My community.

Twenty-eight years ago,
Killed at night.

Looking into the future
I missed out on life.
Young still in high school but
Never was on the scene.

Me, Q, Steel, and Raheem.

You know him
My right hand,
My ace,
My soul.

You know Raheem?
I shot him down cold.
Man, if I was alive?

Would I have grown to be not as
Much of a rebellion?

Would I have grown into a man
Raising my own children?

Would I have grown to except
The truth of the harsh reality of
The pressures of the youth?

Would I have grown closer to my crew?
We were once labeled villains.

Would I have grown apart from
Q who ended up taking my life?

R.O.N

Raheem who I ended up taking his life
Away from his seed.

Would I still be busting Steels chops?
If I didn't attempt to kill my dog.
Leaving him to die in that alley
Laid out to bleed.

Proud of the man Eric aka Steel
Turned out to be, and
Q, I mean Quincy.

I forgive you for killing me.
I only hope when we meet again
You forgive me.
For all of my stupidity.

Twenty-eight years ago
Respect didn't know the ledge living trife.

Steel and Q forgive me, Raheem did.

I miss y'all.
Until we meet again it's
Wrecking crew for life.
Wish I can take the pain away
Through the night.
Only if we could share this
Laughter, if myself
Roland Bishop was alive.

R.O.N

R.O.N

What Would Nip Do?

Waving my blue flag right in
Front of you.
Looking out of my window
Seeing these parallels.

A legend didn't see the
Impact you had on other's
Until your
Untimely demise.
Until your shadow departed
Your soul,
Didn't see your vision,
Didn't realize the enterprise.

That's why we should praise
Our leaders before they pass.
Before the roses die and
The water leaves the glass.

But your spirit is our existence.
A portrait of your image died by
Self-hatred,
Fratricidal existence,
Leaving your children
Fatherless because of a
Broken mirror of sickness.

Waving my blue flag right in
Front of you.

I can show you better than
I can explain it to you.
Was born to be a soldier
Before it was my birth.

R.O.N

Before I was called back home,
Before I departed ways with you from
This hell we call Earth.

A white man's heaven is a
Black man's hell.

Looking outside envisioning turning
L.A. into generational wealth.
In a matrix crucified at 33,
Gunned downed and derailed.

The only thing was missing was
The cross and nails.

They could never stop the beatings
From the heart that won't drop.

Momma,
I'm a legend in a gold frame next to Pac.

When the world ends and this whole
Facade ends up being true.
When the raindrops meet our flesh turning
Our flesh blue.

You'll look beyond the winds,
Beyond the sky,
You'll look above the clouds
Envisioning Nip.

The last of a dying breed
The resurrection of the
Last Crip.

Rest Easy....

R.O.N

R.O.N

H.E.R.O
Hoping Everything Reaches Out

What is a hero?

Someone who reaches out through
The highest capacity?
Someone who holds a crown?
Someone who will fight without a touch?
Someone who is heroic?

Someone in my eye's is a
True King.

Through the good and bad times.
Through the brightness of the sun.
Through the pain of sadness.
You've always encouraged me to
Be great at what I do.
To be #1.

You wear your heart on your sleeve.
Never give up, explore the world.
Go out and achieve.
If you fall, get back up
Don't stop.
If you fall again and bump your head,
Then put some ice on that knot.

Man, big bro
Words can't express what you mean to me.

A poem will turn into a book,
A full fledge story.
When your heartbeats,
My heart beats just as well.

R.O.N

When you cry, I cry.
Just thank the Lord you have
A story to tell.

We give God all praise to the Most High
We give the glory.
The second chapter of your life
Will be your testimony.

I used to question God's motives and asked

"Why you?"

He answered back and said,
Why not you.

Sometimes when you're on a
Constant move,
He will come to humble you.
Now it's time to sit still
My big brother.
My angel on Earth, Heaven sent.
Roses your way to smell the
Beauty of the scent.

Remember the time's when
I was sick?
I was in so much pain as a kid.
You picked me up, literally.

I whispered in your ear,
"Don't let me die, let me live".

See even back then you were a hero to me.
This may sound odd.
But back then you were
More than a hero to me.

R.O.N

You were the closes thing to
God.

My big brother,
This is your little big brother.
Can't wait to hear Leondo,
My middle name out your mouth.

Keep the faith
Big brother, God got this.
The family is here for you.

My H.E.R.O

Hoping Everything Reaches Out

2 U

I Love You Big Bro......
You got this.

> ***Freddy Caldwell***
> ***9/17/1966 ~ 9/30/2021***

R.O.N

R.O.N

A Poem 4 Cat
Catha Jean Caldwell

June 1st 1943
An angel was born into this life.
During an era of segregation,
Racism, lynching's, burning crosses
Set ablaze at night.

God's child here to become
An angel here on earth.
Never overcame the
Hardships of the beatings of our ancestors
Who were hurt.

Your success is so inexpressible
A Queen,
A Woman,
A Sister,
A Mother,
A Grandmother,
A Friend,
An Auntie,
A Cousin.

You've changed the lives of so many
In an abundance.
From the sizzling degrees of Sanford Florida,
To migrating to New York State.

You've took on many jobs, but in
The field of nursing you were great.
But the greatest job you've ever
Took on was like no other.

R.O.N

A black Queen
The strongest of all mothers.
When your soul left us, it was
Like a storm came to visit.
But when the rain became clear,
The son reflected your spirit.

I hope you are looking down
At us and is proud for the most part.

Your heart shall beat again in
Heaven.

God gave you a new start.

Life goes on
You are in the afterlife taking everlasting
Steps to Heaven in paradise.
Dancing with the Supreme being,
And your mother, father, and sisters.
So nice.

June 1st 1943,
An angel was born, naturally strong.
You've earned your wings in
Heaven.

Even though you already had them
Here on Earth.
Seventy-one years long.
We miss you!

> *Catha Jean Caldwell*
> *6/1/1943 ~ 6/19/2014*

R.O.N

R.O.N

A.N.X.I.E.T.Y
Another Night X Illusions Ending Thoughts of Yesterday

Another night of a concussion,
I'm awake living through
These ongoing illusions
That shakes me.
That enters my thoughts
That never ends.
Heartbeats at a drastic pace.
The walls of hell I sit at,
It awaits.

Another night gone to waste.

Why am I so alone?
Why am I so depressingly shattered?
Deserted in a state of
Dismal emptiness.

Why am I so enraged?
Gone one thousand miles away
Anonymously.

X marks the spot of the unknown
The black sheep.
My condition of abnormality,
The conditioning of an
Anomaly.

I need clarity.
Is there a God?
Please help me.

I sit alone in my four-corner room

R.O.N

Not fitting in with the rest of the world,
My mind is an unlit candle.
Razors don't cut through concrete
My heart is made of gold.

Why am I having these angry illusions?
Covered in a costume painted in
Blood trying to come to a
Conclusion.

I need help
I'm feeling like my heartbeat stopped.
Therapist at therapy continues to
Stare at the clock.

Why won't I leave this empty space?
Why won't I believe in myself?
I'm afraid, but afraid of what?

Why am I so afraid?

Blood pressure is high.
I want to live again, the pains of past.
I want to erase
Another night,
    Another night,
        Another sleepless night.
I will get it back.
You asked, what will I get back?
"My life".
Before it blows in the cool breeze.

A.N.X.I.E.T.Y.
Another Night X Illusions
Ending Thoughts of Yesterday.

These are my anxieties.

R.O.N

CHAPTER 4

POEMS IIII

- **R**ighteousness **O**verpowers **N**egligence part 4
- Raindrop Tears
- Priority Prescriptions
- Visions of a Visualizer
- Many Shades of MJ (Massacred Jungle)
- Thunder
- Doomed Child of Confinement
- Target
- A Wise Lion
- Scratching and Surviving

R.O.N
RIGHTEOUSNESS OVERPOWER NEGLIGENCE
PART 4

R.O.N

INHERENT WISDOM

As I still dream on planet Earth,
A ghetto child looking out of
His window staring at the past that
Haunts us.

This is my poem of freedom.
A poem for revolution marked with
Tears of blood engaging at a
Pace so drastically entwined in
The depths of hungry
Lost children.

Feeding their souls through the
Eyes of the wise,
Inherent to the old man's
Wisdom.

As we lay down on a
Permanent mattress
Smelling the fungus of the
Zombies who are
Still alive.

The smoke from the
Crack pipe has the air in
My lungs clogged up with
Maggots and mice.

Ready to exhale the concrete
Can't take no more of the
Burning struggles,
The painted pictures are
Descriptions of life on fire.

R.O.N

I am the noose of the 40's,
The noose hanging from
The bloody trees of the 50's.

I am the bullet of the 60's,
The coke of the 70's,
The crack of the 80's.

Fifty plus years of pain into the 90's
2000's party over, oops out of time.

2020 reaches us through mass destruction.
Hitler's warfare because
We are still burning.
We are still running,
Still fighting in a racist world
Based on religion and creed.

Hellfire awakes in the midst of
A sabotage raged.
Will I pass this bullet down to my seed?

The theories of the manifestation of
The actions we hold
The living vise grip.
Ascertained the truthfulness, but
The ignorance cannot make Allah slip.

Dark mind is in a coma.
This is the spirit of
The essence of the blood of
Tulsa, Oklahoma.

A black wall is being painted on my street.

R.O.N

But I'm too high to see
These visions clearly.
Living for the city on a higher ground,
Staring into the
Soul of the golden lady.

We are in Egypt with Jesus children of
America, all in love is fair.

No war, don't you worry about a thing.
No war, I declare.
Before you stand, first learn how to
Crawl as well as listen.

The so-called leader of the
U.S is Mr. Know-It-All.

These are my inner visions.
This may have gone over your head
As well as the acronym.

R.O.N.

Righteousness
Overpowers
Negligence

Is the emblem.

Inherent Wisdom.

R.O.N

R.O.N

RAINDROP TEARS

Prejudice,
Against intelligent Negros.
Forced to fold in a world that's
Already against a young man.
Already going against the masses.
Already going against the grain.

A simple man holding back the tears.
Stabbed by the
prejudice against intelligent negros.
That's **P.A.I.N**.

Standing in the rain
Black collar popped up,
Deep thoughts visioning dollars thinking change.

Overthrown by fear.

Who are they to judge us?
God is love.
Troublesome from a troubled man,
Raindrop tears.

Back from miles away
Fighting a war
Full of lies in a confused government
Full of negligence.
A threat to this nation,
Rebel without a pause.

In the black steel hour of chaos,
Public enemy #1.
It will take millions to hold us back behind
Trapped bars moved by slave makers,
Politicians, and racist Presidents.

R.O.N

Raindrop tears.

A caption of the rain back from a
War back to the slums.
From a brutal combat,
From a war that doesn't have anything to do with us.

Who am I?

In the inner-city blues
I'm trying.
To proceed in a mistaken unidentified
Place making me wanna' holla.

Trying to control my environment.
Trying to save the children, but
Instead of controlling my environment,
I became that product,
That victim bottled up with
Depression.

Trouble at home,
Trouble in the ghetto stressing,
Trouble everywhere I look,
Trouble seems to follow
Me.

The late 60's, early 70's a party with
Panthers after X,
After the assassination of our
Glorious King.

Right on my brother.
Can I call you, my brother?
Is calling out to you that hard.
Our religion has faded away,

R.O.N

The wholly holy has
Vanished from our God.

Still searching battling in our lifetime,
Sitting on a cloud with
Wings and a halo, and down under
There is a picture of the world in despair.

Sitting on a cloud in a chair,
Staring at my reflection with
Horns, bats, and snakes, a serpent of
A destructive force, but does anybody care?

So, I abuse my mind away,
God's creative temple is fried.
Since returning home from the
Prejudice against intelligent negros
Became another tragic jewel
Flying high in the
Friendly skies.
An early demise.

Pride now,
I'm forced to move back home
With momma.

Never thought I would
Succumb by the hands of my own father.
When I woke up after my death,
I was hugged through
Protection of our father

God,
Please save me.
Mercy,
Mercy
Me.

R.O.N

What's going on in a
World filled with problems,
Feeling like you will
Never grow or succeed.

So, I ask watch over
My babies,
I'm ready to leave.

Heavenly Father,
Please take me.
I did the best I could,
Nobody understood.

These *raindrop tears.*

R.O.N

R.O.N

PRIORITY PRESCRIPTIONS

I feel like,
I'm in the middle of something
Real ignorant.

Placed in the middle then,
Looking at these defeated pyramids.
Prison or death shouldn't be
The only option for our children.

Now they prey upon the weak,
Innocent babies leak blood and
Blue is after you.

Bad or good.

That's a long walk from that
Alley even Ricky got hit by
Them boyz in the hood.

Kill or be executed.

Is there a reasonable doubt?
The air I'm feeling it, D'evil is prepared
To bring it on these politics as usual,
For these dead Presidents.

Cutty will pistol whip you down them stairs.
Ain't no nigga here just a struggling
Black poet with eloquence of
Cashmere thoughts.

Can't knock the hustle though.
Trying not to bend but under pressure
I feel lost.

R.O.N

My little partner is depressed,
Says he's coming of age.
Twenty- two with his first born on its way.

I was twenty-two too
When my son seen this dark page.
The only thing you can do is
Prepare them for the worse,
While trying not to see an early grave.

Watch your circle.
Which way is up?
Decide which way you want to go.

The ones who are around you,
Will be the ones that will hiss and bite you,
Friend or foe.

Can I live in peace?
Can I escape the dark blue sea?

That turned into dark black, that separated itself,
From the beautiful ocean and breeze.

When it's all over,
Bury me in black and white, with a brim hat, and
With a cigar in my hand.

I lived with no regrets.

Only want to sit on the bench
With shorty of the youth, is that an object?

A young, defeated child, who feels there is
No realistic hope,
That he'll make it out of the projects.

R.O.N

Twelve going on twenty,
Messing with guns,
Trying to educate on the real war, and
To be prepared.

You see them on the corner.
They'll be out here forever,
On them same stairs.
You got to know when
The smoke clears, how to strike.

Mad brothers are dying on them same corners.
You don't want that to be you right?
Rise above the madness, mind elevation,
You got Jewell's
Not only in your pocket, but upstairs.

We are facing unquestionable times.
Just stay ready for the mark of the
Beast that lies in the belly!

R.O.N

R.O.N

VISIONS OF A VISUALIZER

This life after,
You can't escape it.
This world will leave you naked,
No one is sacred.
Some people ain't your family,
They are just related.
A bunch of squares in that round hole.
Empty minded peers.

Still in my prime, but
Celebrating brotherhood with
My brother of forty years.

Don't let that go over your head know
We still suffering from losing our best friend.
Trying to escape the pain, but
Ending up back where we began.

Voice of the voiceless.
I don't think no one is listening.

What you know about seeing your mother pass?
Defecating on herself, coughing up blood.
I still feel some sense of release
From settling our differences.

The mind is tricky, we compete in a
Genocidal plantation often.

Ain't nothing like the pain of seeing the lady
Who kept you warm,
Not talking and laying in a coffin.

She told my brother look out for me.
Nothing is promised.

R.O.N

She knew her last baby would be
The one to hurt the hardest.
Smelled betrayal standing in front of me.

Make a wish.
I wish for peace over war in a
Zone of fratricidal existence.
We all gotta answer to the
Most High someday.
Enter the gate.

Moms' physical is gone and had people
Turn on during my vulnerable state.

I'll love you from a distance
Before I let another violate.

Keep the wicked far away,
Do not entertain the circus.

If you do
You might as well keep a red nose, and
Big boots near your surface.
Nervous, but visioned war from the start.
Anxiety but fear cannot overpower a brave heart.

Mind is sharp,
The uncivilized is in a deep coma.
Married to fashion and wealth,
Blood diamonds still rule.
The Goddess is a distraction, you can't
Bury vanity with you.

This is the life we chose.
I'm just a beautiful substance.
Rather stand from a far,
Then fall from grudges.

R.O.N

Holding on to the winds.
Can you stand the rain when it pours?

A heartbreak that's new can
Devour you and yours.

How did it come to this?

Two stepping on the Devils dance floor,
Drinking Satan's piss.
Poisoning are mind's, nauseous, can't stand firm.
Every man for himself in a place
That's already burned.

We are quick to defend the guilty, but
Castrate the innocent.

Free my nigg, well you know the rest.
But that same man you want free
He done just killed again.
Then he got killed, but you defended him.

My baby was a sweet child,
Who would give the shirt off of
His back fast.

The same baby who was set free,
The same baby who ended up
Letting another gun blast.

If you don't humble yourself
The lambs will be silenced.
A sacrificial slaughter.
Knowledge and righteous moves against all.
That's Karma.

R.O.N

R.O.N

MANY SHADES OF M.J MASSACRED JUNGLE

A Black man covered in a
White world, seems like
I'm always lying on my side.

State of shock in
The middle of a dark street,
With five black brothers by my side,
Preparing to get sucked by
The dark blue sky.

But through victory, my right palm glows.
Can you feel it?

I'm a giant in the sky,
Sprinkling the children of a
Lesser God.

The ways to free the mind.

Six black brothers, that
Six can turn into ten,
Ten turning into
A million-man march.
A million black men.
A million in a nation,
You can't hold us back.
We all could win.
A black body,
Skin is made of black leather.

R.O.N

Stomping the Black streets with
A lightening spark.
When I touch it, it glows.

The black tiger,

The black onyx,

The black seal.

A kiss from a rose,
7th day scroll the judgement,
The instructions have been unveiled.

A black body,
Regardless the pigmentation of
My skin.

A black body,
Alone in the dark, eventually lost
My brother's.

The perfect plan to separate
Me from my kin.
So, I walk the streets
Alone in red blood.

The metal hits both of my shoulders,
Traveling down to my chest.
Blood and metal, zipped up in pieces.
I rest.

Beat it, your heart pumps in
The middle of the night,
Blood is covered on one black piece.

We are the world, monsters,

R.O.N

Demonic scavengers dancing in the streets.
They hate us.
They don't really care about us.
Prisons and blood pools is
A black bodies future wherever you're at.
Many shades of a massacred jungle, but
The shade is traced black.
The color remains red,
A black body remains black.
The land was green,
The sky rained snow then
A black body was under attack.

I was placed here.
Momma gave birth to
Six black babies,
Six black bodies who may not live to
See the light of day.
Six bodies imagined in the creation of
A bronze-colored complexion.
The many shades of a black body,
Spare his warm heart.
The degrees of a massacre in the
Jungle is prominent.
In the jungle we gravitate towards
The sickness of violence.

Where am I going with this poem?
Where am I going with this writing?
Where am I going with this piece of painting?

The many shades of a
Colored man in 2021 is frightening.
The streets is all I know or

R.O.N

Should I say the choices we make.
A smooth criminal savage cannot break.
Gotta' look at my reflection,
Man in the mirror.
You can't see clearly
Through the thick fog.
Every day is dangerous,
Bad circumstance in this here concrete jungle.
Gotta' get my back from off the wall.

I keep losing my brothers,
Kin folk or not.
I keep envisioning
Black bodies at the core they rot.

Is the jungle a masquerade?

False pretense!
God makes no mistakes.
Fed to the wolves, they think they're in an
Invincible space.
Woke up from this illusion,
Watching the streets.

It was all a dream.

Escaped the madness of
The ghetto life,
Turning nightmares into dreams.
Had a nightmare of killing myself and
My brothers in the jungle.
Falling down the eternal stairway,
Fire over my head.
I'm a poet and this is all I know.
I don't wanna' kill my brother anymore.
I want us to live!

R.O.N

R.O.N

THUNDER

An angel with dirty wings.
Can you feel the
Hopelessness?
The anguish?
The Earths severe stroke,
The heart disease of the youth's adolescence.
Swallowed up by that black hole,
The illness of the world,
Trying to find a place to regain
My strength through
Convalescence.

My presence gift wrapped
The curse.

The 3rd month, 9th day
Was the writings of a dark birth.

The world is over, yup.
New world order.

And gaining freedom better chance at
Pampering a Cobra.
Black Panthers spirit.

We living in one big movie.
Directed by Shayton.
We carrying out his ritual duties.

I said it's miserable in the jungle.
Do you agree?

Yes? Lying. No.

R.O.N

Am I recovering where the
Thunder skies roar?
The destination of a last
Fatal conquest.

A destructive force has erupted.
I can feel it to the core.
Can't disregard the fact that
The wolf is at the door.

The beast marked me
Eighteen times total.
It's marked for death,
In the eyes of the enemy.
There is no trust.

God's descended jewel plummet but
Got back up.

A wild cat feeling the
Pressures of ignominy.
The fresh scent of a panther strikes.

I'm a tiger,
Faster than a cheetah
Roaming the bush at night.
In a climate where everything is
Seized by corruption and greed.

Taking bites of my martyrs,
Snarfed down my enemies.

I am Earth, eunuch.
I am the bitterness that
Lies in the sky.
Transformed into a bloody hurricane, castrated,
Sending signals to the blind.

R.O.N

I am still living!

Fire of war is my disguise.
He lives in darkness.
Been dead more than he's been
Alive.

Wrap my body in cloth.

Organs play…..

I am no longer left.
Preserve my body in
The afterlife or in death.

Welcome to Earth!

R.O.N

R.O.N

DOOMED CHILD OF CONFINEMENT

They send
US to US to destroy
US and if US work with
US instead of working against
US.
Then there wouldn't be any
Integration -VS - segregation and more
Determination amongst
US we are segregated from
US.

My own kind killed me in the cold.
Blood own
Then left my soul to be captured out in
The snow.

Hale hits my skin in Hell.
I inhale the imprisoned
Cells that glooms.

Fall into a systematic trap,
Might sprain my ankle, as
I fell, spring up into a garden that's doomed.

Hot days awaits.
Some more past, some more go.
Wind tares the air as
The rain blows.

No pretty colors in the sky,
Only Negros with guns.
The impotence of solitude
Through a vigorous circumstance
Has only just begun.

R.O.N

The leaves are blackened.
The trees turned into dust,
Captured the rain, bow hits the solar,
Losing my identity inside
The sun.
Atoms split,
Traveling at right speed.

Fruit of life,
It's bittersweet underneath that tree.
This is a bitter winters eve.
The coldest storm ever created
By Mother Nature.
She lives.

Got my body cold as ice,
Feeling like the lost of a chilled soul.

Inside my own cell,
I feel impregnable to the world, but
Still feels like an empty rib.

Cage bird sings the blues,
Wishing that he could escape
These steel walls,
Turning iron into glass.

To breathe life back into
The shattered ruins of the past.
The devil tried to inject me but
God protected me in
His daughter's womb.
Came out opened my eyes,
Cried looking up into this bright light.
Cried to go back into the womb.

R.O.N

A tear suddenly turned
Into laughter.

Direction into the son,
Then another
Tear turned into a black moon.

An infant placed here to roast,
Beef here in a pile of snow.

White Amerikkka, private property.
Along with the chickens and goats.

The alienated slave standing near
Uncle Tom's cabin.
Still confined in his own mine
Still searching for life, liberty, and
The pursuit of happiness.

We are asked to die for
The system in the middle east.

The same system back home,
Where we are executed in the streets.
Systematically trapped.

Four seasons came and went
For ME.
For US. Hate used on
US by US
For US to keep US behind those
Frozen walls, only US.
The hate you give
Got me not standing the sight of
The slave master's blood.

R.O.N

Gone in the smoke in
The flames of fire.

A prisoner in my own
Mental state of being,
Entombed
Extensive,
More than four days
Lazarus!

Doomed Child of Confinement.

R.O.N

R.O.N

TARGET

They *killed* Malcolm,
They *killed* our King.
They *killed* Christ image,
They *killed* all our leaders.
And the way we are supposed to think.

Guilty until proven innocent
Where is the equality.
Even when the proof is in the sand,
You're still guilty.
In a subverted environment
We sweep everything under the rug.
Still chains unbreak.

Impoverished with a vessel of hope
They destroy our physical being
Through the ways of incompetence.
Just because your eyes are
Open don't mean
That you're awake.

Guilty until proven innocent.
In time I'm suspended.
Why argue with the blind
They can't see your
Vision.

They *killed* our musicians,
They *killed* M.J,
They *killed* Prince,
They *killed* Cosby,
They *killed* Dr. Sebi
They are *killing* our spiritual healing.

R.O.N

Targets they do it all the time.
Cosby gets caged in?

Do this then;
Charge Weinstein for the same crime.
When the light shines,
They assassinate more than our character.
Give a black man the power

They *kill* us all the time.
Authority, they abuse it.

Prince!
They destroyed him
Still stood through bravery.
Slave symbolizes
The sick corporate contracts equating
The system to slavery.

M.J!
They destroyed the King.
For years he was under attack.

Sony!
He wanted to depart because of the lies and
Stealing of money from artist who were black.

Mr. Cosby,
Was plotted on and tarnished.
They destroyed his reputation,
Clearly a conspiracy.
While they're whispering in the dark,
We'll *kill* that nigger dead before we let him
Buy NBC.

R.O.N

It's corruption!
Life of desperation holding on
To hope in a hopeless place,
We unfurl.
Waiting on the day for this
World to break my children's heart so
They can really see the ways of
The world.

Anytime you become that product of
A voice through visibility.
We come up missing.

Painted the color brutal
Through a vague imagery.

Give us enough money, we'll decompose.
You can't see these visible steps?

They're *killing* our future leaders.

Wake up!!

Or

You will be next!

R.O.N

R.O.N

A WISE LION

A baby lion was trapped in a cage,
In a lion's den.

Cocaine let down.

Suffocating in the jungle,
I can't breathe.
A lion losing oxygen,
Lost in the jungle all alone.

Everywhere I look there are
Animals with
Blood and saliva
Dripping from their mouths.

A baby cub must hold his own.
A cub walking the
Jungle of cocaine freely,
With another cub trying to escape
The dark parade that I feel is
Hunting me.

I'm captured by my hunter,
The result from wanting to
Follow the other cubs.

Now I'm confused melting in a
Cocaine pot,
Surrounded by other cubs.
Looking at my owner.
Looking him dead in his eyes.

As a young cub,
I can feel the hatred he has for

R.O.N

Me and I don't know why.

My owner beat me up.
I'm just a baby
Forced in a cage.
Crying heart can't understand the
Development of the
Hunter's rage.

As a baby cub,
I am still imagining growing into a lion,
The king of the jungle.

But a lion is a lost cub
Still breathing the smell of
Cocaine's trouble.

Locked in imprisonment,
A baby can't escape in fear
Trapped in a cage of prison
Not knowing what awaits.

This is my story of an enslaved cub.

Captured from Africa
400 plus years ago,
Still swimming trying not to drown,
Walking on dry cracked blood.

I need vindication.
From this conviction, from an unjust
Incarceration.
I'm trying to be the best that I can be.
I'm trying to defeat anxiety.
Trying to escape my reality.

R.O.N

For a decade plus
I fought and
I fought and
I fought.
Putting up a fight.

Until I was set free back in the jungle,
AKA the ghetto of
Cocaine America.
Resurrected into a King's lion named
King Wise.

That was me a cub thousands of
Years ago, formed into a
Lion's King.

Earned my crown
An activist, advocating to reform
The criminal injustice
Amongst us.

Traveling the country sharing my story.
A wise lion with the world in
Both of my palms.

The other cub whom
I walked the jungle with was my friend
Another lion transformed into
Yusef Salaam.

Remember my name,
Remember the times.
Remember the youth's innocence
Was taken away.
Remember the golden eyes
That shines when they see us.
Remember one thing.

R.O.N

When they see us,
Remember
I've been exonerated but
A lion isn't
Free.

Remember me!

R.O.N

R.O.N

SCRATCHING & SURVIVING

Pissy staircases,
Broken elevators,
Holes in the walls.
Rats and roaches crawl,
They cover us all.

Tenement buildings,
Abused children, burned with hot irons.
Mentally damaged,
Drug addicted black mommas.

Just looking out of the window,
Watching the days go by.
Making a wave when you can, in the ghetto.
Layoffs aren't temporary.
Keep your head above water.
Rip-offs is easy credit if necessary.

Mad dog bullets hit from a 22,
20/20 hits the liver, a saint in the night.

Red flag around my head,
Walking the slums isn't an option.
Walking in my enemies territory and
Start poppin'.

Trying to dodge Pops speeches.
The circumstances of a kid in the ghetto is hard.
Trying to scratch and survive.
Trying not to break my
Momma's heart.

Poor and poverty don't mix.
Well, believe this.

R.O.N

Thinking my luck runs deep,
Staring in the blood shot eyes of a
Black Jesus.

A portrait of a piece painted
Descriptively by yours truly of
A child who's trying to manage.

I'm a work of art.
Painting pictures on canvases.
Turning winos into prophets.
Gotta' teach the young, gifted, and black
How to deal with the pressures of the slums.

Black and I'm proud, yep
Young, and gifted.
Poor righteous teacher.
Wise intelligent but yet militant.

Others can't hear me,
There is black with beauty.

Intelligent hoodlum feel the
Awakening of a tragedy.
My sister wants to be a professional dancer.
Trying to make it out of this hellhole.

Ended up married with children,
But she escaped the ghetto.

Looking back, there was a bunch of
Hard times and problems.
As momma pray for a better way,
Waiting for the neighborhood gossip
From the next-door neighbor.
Her lips always filled with rumors and lies.

R.O.N

As momma listens
As she stands by the stove,
As she stirs the hot oatmeal.

Pop's is agitated.
He just got laid off again.
Money is low, and on the door reads
Eviction.

Notice the man of the house always
Has pride and only
He knows how
He feels inside.
Can't sleep at night trying not to worry
The wife and on top of that not eating right.
Plus, his blood pressure is
Extremely high.

Just looking out of the window
Watching the day's go by.
Pinching for a penny.

Abused child futures looking empty.

Just looking out of the window,
Watching the days go by.
Pops died in a tragic car accident,
As we still scratch and survive.

Whoever heard of good times?

CHAPTER 5

R.O.N

POEMS V

- **R**ighteousness **O**verpowers **N**egligence part 5
- Who Am I To Speak?
- Leftovers
- The Big Piece of Chicken
- Mixed Emotions
- P.O.P.S (Property Oppressed Persecuted Slave)
- I Wonder
- Uncivilized Wisdom
- Goddess Image
- Purple Reign

R.O.N
RIGHTEOUSNESS OVERPOWER NEGLIGENCE
PART 5

R.O.N

TILL THIS DAY

I am Cassius,
Getting bullied before he learned
How to protect himself.

I am Muhammad Ali,
The greatest of all time, who inspired
Generations to come.

I am Jack Johnson,
With a mink on with two white women
By my side, who inspired Ali.

Our history
I envisioned with pride.

I am Duke Ellington,
Louie, Count Basie,
Cab Calloway at the cotton club
Looking lavish in zoot suits.

I am Lena Horne,
Miss Fitzgerald, Miss Dandridge,
Billie Holliday side by side in pursuit.

I am a young King,
A confused child not understanding
The pitfalls of racism in the 30's.

I am Dr. King's
I have a dream speech of the 60's.

I am Dr. King,
Laying in a puddle of blood on a balcony.

R.O.N

I am Malcolm Little,
Birthed in Omaha Nebraska.
I am Detroit Red,
Playing no games, a hustler.

I am Malcolm X,
A leader with a cause,
By any means necessary.

I am Malcolm X,
Assassinated in Harlem in the 60's.

I am Kaepernick,
Kneeling on one knee.

I am the preacher,
The teacher,
The revolt leader hanging from a tree.

I am the God,
Searching for the last pyramid on a chariot.

I am the beginning,
Of the railroad underground,
That really wasn't underground.

I am Harriet.
I am Nina Simone,
Being misunderstood.
I am the black household,
The bad and the good.

I am the past, future, and the present.

I am Afeni Shakur,
Giving birth to a legend.
I am Langston Hughes,

R.O.N

An American poet, scriptures are written.

I am Irish blood,
Mixed with African roots of
My past is embedded in me.
I am the sun, moon, and stars
I am reality.

I am the illmatic cover,
A young boy with the project living
Shadowed in the back of me.

I am Miles Davis,
Voice smooth but scary.
I'll be back round about midnight.

I am Donny Hathaway,
Before jumping off that building
Taking his own life.
I am the homeless being ignored
By the rich.

I am that same homeless man
Who overcame adversity.
A reflection in the wind.

I am a portrait of a boy,
Interrupted by a man who frequently
Self-absorbs himself in the mirror.
I am Quincy Jones,
Conceptually thinking of
Thriller.

I am the beginning to an end,
The fireworks in the sky.

R.O.N

I am the incarcerated Scarface,
Rehabilitated the imprisoned mind.
I am a father to a son who is better than I.

My offspring at its best.

I am the last fighter, fighting to the death.
I live to learn.
Thinking of the Kings and Queens
Who came before me.

The ones I mentioned in this poem
I salute and praise.

I am Deontay Wilder's,
Right hand.

R.O.N.

Righteousness Overpowers Negligence

TILL THIS DAY!

R.O.N

. R.O.N

WHO AM I TO SPEAK?

My 3rd eye,
Has seen the glory and many other things.
Still waiting for the land that was
Promised by a
King.

On a mountaintop I write,
Another picture I paint.
While my ancestor's blood is injected in my veins.

This isn't me speaking,
This is the slave who tried to
Escape the one who tried to run fast,
Trying to stay alive.

This isn't me speaking,
This is the solider with whips on
His back.

No glory just a brave heart with a
Tear in his eye.

This isn't me speaking,
This is the spirit of a child hung
Down by the river.

This isn't me speaking,
This is the body on the pavement,
Burned to a crisp while
Devilish grins point fingers.

This isn't me speaking,
This is the ancestral slave.

R.O.N

This isn't me speaking,
This is the spirits of black souls
Heads sticking out from their graves.

This isn't me speaking,
This is Bob Marley anointing my body.

This isn't me speaking,
This is a black poet from
The 16th century, probably.

This isn't me speaking,
This is Nat Turner's frustration.
Kill or be killed.

This isn't me speaking,
This is the steel hearts of men.

This isn't me speaking,
This is the image of Emmett's picture
With the fedora before things got critical.

This isn't me speaking,
This is the angelic voice of
Mahalia Jackson before
King's burial.

This isn't me speaking,
This is the precious Lord
Taking my hand.

This isn't me speaking,
This is the skin of the children
Executed on stolen land.

This isn't me speaking,
This is the ideology of a philosophical thinker.

R.O.N

MOVE!

This isn't me speaking,
This is the anger clearly in depth,
40 years a prisoner.

This isn't me speaking,
This is if poverty had a voice and angles
I keep hitting them.

This isn't me speaking,
This is the dead end of a failed system.
This isn't me speaking,
This is the war I declare.

This isn't me speaking,
This is El Hajj Malik Shabazz on
His back gasping for air.
This isn't me speaking,
This is the red summer massacre speaking.

Who am I to speak?

I'm just another Negro
Who died again with his brains leaking.

This isn't me speaking,
This is my momma's southern
Stories embedded within.
This isn't me speaking,
This is the weapons and shields
To use against the snakes with wings
Representing paganism, but

Who am I to speak?

R.O.N

R.O.N

LEFTOVERS

How do we turn nothing into plenty?

How do we shake the stereotypes
That was created by the loser?

The enslavement winner.
How do we turn slavery into sugar?
The taste of the fried chicken,
Collard greens, baked mac & cheese,
Cornbread, the taste of the soul.
The leftovers smell.

The replacement of the seasoning
Has faded away from the alpha male.

The black keys on the piano,
The baseline drums is us.
The ink from the pen we spill to
Cook through happiness and
Sadness is all the way us.

Us all the way us,
Everything and then some, of what
We got on our dinner plate.
Southern comfort.
Walking the pavements literally,
Where Trayvon took his fate.

Impactful power.
Here's the seasoning for the gumbo.
People change like the seasons.
The leftovers.

R.O.N

Oprah stop being Sofia a long time ago.

It's deeper than the
Self of knowledge, start living.
Rather be a chosen of God,
Than to a society that's a secret.

I am my momma's ingredients in
Her baked mac & cheese,
Aunties baked beans,
The yams, plus the barbeque.
The sugar in the Kool-Aid,
The everything that'll eventually kill you.
The swine intestines,
The chitterlings in the dish.
The hush puppy when I'm running from my owner.
The preparing of the fish took nothing,
Made it platinum while in the caged trapped.
Took nothing made something when
The owners threw us scraps.

Me:
I was the house Negro,
But still a slave.
Daddy said I was born into slavery, and
Everything I am set to do in life
Will disperse.

Don't matter if I have a drop of
The white man's blood you're still a curse.
So go ahead eat your death away.
Be like your mammy's side of
The family.

R.O.N

Clean that plate, you can't escape.
Boy it's real, this hate.
But I am the spirit of the soul until
I am no longer.

We are the food that captivates
The heart that they tried to
Throw away.

DAMN!

They could care less for
The leftovers.

R.O.N

R.O.N

THE BIG PIECE OF CHICKEN

Wake up child!

No exception to the rules.
Wake up!
I said, wake up!

Time for school,
Put on your jacket.
Outside as you can feel
It's a little cold.

I don't want to go to school!
It ain't about what you want.
It's about what the future holds.
Birds are chirping, grass is wet.

Do you know what endangered species mean?

His reply, no.
It basically means that you are a threat.

A threat?

Yeah, a threat.

An animal in their eyes.
You see when you are a threat to society
They will throw you in prison.
But when you're a threat to
The world you become an extinction.
A risk.
A loser.

Everything you do you will fail.
You're a bigger threat when

R.O.N

You're educated.

The street thug isn't much of
The problem because they'll end up
Dead or in jail.

My only begotten son reply was
"I'm only ten."

I repeated, "only?"

Well ten is when the experimentation begins.
And it's very scary.

"What does experimentation mean?"

He asked as he picks up his wrestling figure.
I said.

"Put Rey Mysterio down and grab the dictionary."

He sucks his teeth, and rolls his eyes,
Not knowing what awaits, is danger.
A massacre.

But who is going to teach our children
How to move in White America?

They frown upon our men,
From the womb, from birth.

There is an infant mortality that
Begins at birth.

How do we raise us to be strong?
In a land crushed with less Imani tactics, and
More nefarious activities.

R.O.N

Wicked ways to be left in a
Land with no responsibilities.

Remember what I taught you at four
What is bad?

He answered, "guns are bad."
Yeah, life lessons.

Guns are bad and can be more
Harmful if they're not used with
The right direction.

Fast forward.

Never thought I'd see the day
My first born would pick up a gun,
All I ever wanted to do was educate.

The scene of the movie, when
He throws rocks in the ocean?

Not the many black boys in the hood,
The fathers who are there, yelling

> "PUT DOWN THE MOTHERFUCKING
> GUN TREY!"

He loves his son, only wanted to see
The development from within.
I gave you them wings
Go fly.

The choices you make are your own.
I can't bail you out of prison.

Never wanted to fit that high percentage of

R.O.N

The high rate of being absent.

Separated from the black household,
Thought I'll be the one to break those chains.
But instead feeling the anxiety of you being
Taught by whomever remains.

The father loves his son, as he should.

He only tried to self-educate.
Did not want to see you being a high risk, and
Prime candidate of not entering manhood.

Your 5th grade teacher said,
You or your classmates will fail the standardized test.
In a room full of black children.

In other words what she wanted to say
That half if not all of your future looks dim.

So, they place us in remedial classes.
That will eventually turn into
Special Education.
Then label the children hyperactive with
the form of hypertension.

To drug us at an early age.
Drugging us with a controlled substance
That'll give our babies, our children
Irregular heartbeats in the form of
Ritalin.

Yes, son they already
See you and other black infants

R.O.N

As fatherless children.

Not saying I was perfect, but what do I know?

All I ever was, quote on quote was a

"Dead Beat Dad"

Who only worked hard for

The big piece of chicken.

R.O.N

R.O.N

MIXED EMOTIONS

I HATE YOUR GUTS!!!

That's what my emotions use to tell me.

What was it, the self-hatred?

Looking at the color of my skin.
What am I black or white?

l hate myself because I don't know thyself.
Hate breeds jealousy amongst so called
People who aren't friends.

Freckled faced, half breed,
High yella', mixed breed, oreo.

Lost with no place to go.
Mom left me alone to view the minstrel show.
Looking at the misplaced direction of the
African American in the 19th century.

Europeans lampooned blacks as being
Buffoons with ongoing buffoonery.
Labeled as a race as, dimwitted and lazy.

Cannot express it enough,
I'm lost.

I'm so FUCKING LOST!!!

Weary, all alone.
Mommy use to think I was embarrassed
Because of her size and skin tone.

R.O.N

She use to tell me as an infant,
That the stares, were crazy.
She use to say people looked as if to say,
What in the world is this
Dark skinned woman doing carrying this white baby?

Try and swallow that pill.

Mixed emotions.

Envisioning the thought process of how
Bob Marley would feel.
In my other life I was the baby who was
A descendant of slavery.

Mother lived on her knees,
Using her hands to feed another baby of
The other race,
Teaching them as if they were
The seed.

This is the house that was never built.

I tried to escape but was thrown back in
The house
While mother was
Whipped back in the field.

Nigger run!

You shall be killed by the blink of a spark.

The unwanted race, many have died
Young and uneducated not knowing
Who they are.

R.O.N

That was me always seeing
The worst of things.

Pessimistic.

I was sick so I ran from the medication.
Now as I look into the mirror,
I have beaten the odds.

Now as I look into the mirror.
I see the reflection of God.
Mirror images, self-preservation.

I am a King buried in the
Sands of Egypt.

A warrior was at his proudest
Moments of peace asleep eternally in a
Tomb near my Goddess.

A puzzle no longer missing a piece.
No longer a descendant of slavery,
But a descendant of

O.M.A.D

Organization of Men of an African Descent.

Mixed Emotions.

R.O.N

R.O.N

P.O.P.S
PROPERTY OPPRESSED
PERSECUTED SLAVE

They say
I'm property.
I'm oppressed.
I'm persecuted, a slave.

In Amerikkka.

Yes, persecuted since my birth date in 1928.
They say I'm hopeless.
Like a penny with a hole in it.
My story. Well, here is more.

I was drafted by the government
To fight in the Korean war.
Literally seen blacks burned and tortured.

Smell the seasoning on the leaves.
As chocolate covered fruit bodies
Swung from trees.

A teenager trying to escape
The brutal combat that's mistakenly as
Confused as the world out there.

In a place where I could easily be
The next fragrance.
The death scent of the aroma swinging in
The air.

R.O.N

So, is it a mortal combat?
But who wins?
Fighting in a war who won't fight for us,
This war shouldn't exist.

Korean babies blown into bits.
Mothers trading sexual
Advances for chocolate.

It's like royalty to them, and I had plenty.

Planted my seeds.
I want to leave this dark hole.
Smell the odor of death through
The walls of savagery.

Oppressed and persecuted property.

A slave in a war that they declared is
No surprise.
The hate never ceases.
Still can remember the face of
Hitler when he was alive.

Not our fight.

I was only seventeen when he died.
Even though that was a different war,
But they are all
The same.

They all glorify and symbolize
The mural of
Hate.

Well, I survived the Korean war,
Plenty of chapters to this page.

R.O.N

Have I really escaped the war on racism and segregation?

I'm full of jokes and laughter, but
Deep inside there will always be
Everlasting pain.

Now I'm just
A black man,
A hard worker in White Amerikkka,
And best believe in it.
I've worked damn hard.

In 89' separated from my sons' mom.
He was eleven then,
Probably was confusing to him,
He loves his mother, but
His choice was to lay next to Pops.

Taught him everything I know.

I see you above the clouds,
In the clouds I see everything.
Proud of you son, and
The man you've become.

Me, a country western man.

As a black man, I've been through it all.
A black man with a portrait of
Dolly Parton framed on my kitchen wall.

Cruising the scene with my fisherman hat,
Watching the sun flash.
With my son on the passenger side.

R.O.N

Window's down halfway,
On a hot summer day
Telling my past stories,
Listening to Johnny Cash.

Son I know you miss me.
I miss you too.
You don't know the half of
The pain I had to
Endure.

Just understand that
As a black man,

I don't have to suffer anymore.

Pop's will always be here.

R.O.N

R.O.N

I WONDER

I wonder
Why we are still here, trapped in a cage?

Singing the blues.
Segregated at birth but
Still, I sing.
Still, I rise.
Still, I fly an angel with broken wings.
Hungry.
Unfulfilled.
Losing weight.
Separated from the preacher,
Wondering why he continues to
Rob the collection plate.

I wonder,
Why so many kids are dying in my city?

I wonder,
Why this opioid epidemic is so crazy?

I wonder if the mayor cares.
Does the mayor have any sympathy?

I wonder,
Why mom spirit keeps on protecting me?

People I looked at as family
Don't realize their life was on the line.
Standing over them with a knife.
I couldn't do it.
I couldn't put up a fight.

R.O.N

It took God and fear not to kill him,
That night!

I wonder,
If our music is just an illusion?

It could've been another tool to
Express ourselves through
Music.
The calm before the storm

Where is the resolution?
After the knee what is the solution?

I wonder,
What if Scarlett was Nefertiti?
What if Egyptian prophets were
Still alive?

Tombstones still stand strong.
Africa still has its pride.

Do you ever wonder
What this world would be like
Without crack cocaine?

How it wouldn't have got inside of
Rick James veins?

What happened to Richard Pryor's thoughts?
How was his memory lost?

I'm **wondering** for a second.
What happened when he went through the fire?
When it burned the legend.

R.O.N

What did he see first when he entered God's kingdom?
Was Redd Foxx there jokingly to greet him?

I wonder,
Why our birthday is transformed into death.

I wonder,
Why I reached for a star but fell with regrets?

In the real world a change gonna' come.
It's due.
Impeach the President
The voice is us.

I wonder,
If our evolution will enter?

I can still hear the cries from the ghosts of
Our ancestors.
Our leaders' wounds healed.
Shots came and went.
Flowers over their caskets perished.
Heaven sent an angel,
But racism still exist.
They don't want to see us win.
We are living
Underneath the cement through
Tenement buildings,
Overlooking plantations.

I wonder,
If this art form will go back to its culture?
Or
Will it take its last breath?

R.O.N

Is it over?

I wonder,
Why mom had to go and take her last ride.

I wonder,
Why my cousin told me she took her own life,
Like my feelings don't matter.

Still, I rise.

I wonder,
Why he pulled a gun on my mother.
We can go far
With a conversation.
If he would have shot her dead thirty years ago,
Who would have raised me?

I was going through my own transformation.

DAMN!

I WONDER!

R.O.N

R.O.N

UNCIVILIZED WISDOM

She used to be essential.

Beauty turned out by the beast
So monumental.
Lost in the wind
Love turned into pain.

Queens turned into Jezebels.
Words captivated she's drained.

I pray she enters back my wisdom.

Heartbroken by her backbone
Lord forgive them.
She's confused with no place to go.
So, she sales her body for cash to get blow.

Babies at home, no proper guidance.

Intelligence,
She lacks to be honest.
Could've been in
College studying the world.
A continuous cycle through
The soul of her baby girl.

Uncivilized woman.

Wisdom betrayed, cold.
All she wanted in life was
A father to hold.
Misguided in this world
Full of mistakes.

R.O.N

Black child
An unfortunate waste.

I wanted to rescue you away
From the madness.
But you'd rather stay
Blindfolded.
Pure sadness.
Staying loose,
So confused,
So innocent.

Uncivilized wisdom.

You are so beautiful,
So, blessed.
Don't know the reason you're
Half-naked and depressed inside.

So, she tries to ignore the purpose
So, she hides.

Three seeds,
Three different baby daddies

It's common.

No support from none of them
It's all so common.

Inhale this
Earth as you
Exhale impure air.
Gain your knowledge,
Look in the mirror.
A Goddess is in there.

R.O.N

Get up!
Stop laying on your back.
Promiscuous.
You could be more than that.

Time is of the essence.
Time don't waste.

If not for your own,
At least for your kid's sake.

My backbone needs to
Come back home
Realistically.
Emotionally scared.
Through life's impurities.

Uncivilized wisdom.

We were once
Kings by our Queens
We stood strong,
On our land called
Our Mother.
We couldn't do no wrong.
Stripped from
Our own homes,
Our continent is crucial.

Now in the coming of
Our father it's critical.

Egyptian Goddess
Her spirit lies from within.
Breathtaking Genesis. I gave you a rib.

R.O.N

Pathological liars killed
Our history.
Impregnated my mother throughout slavery.
Beat her,
Raped her,
Hung her in the dark woods.

Strange fruit.

Now we are misguided.
That's such a bad look.
Made Mother dance in the jungle.
Back bruised.

Today,
Formed into prostitution.
Over the clouds
I'm formed into a bird.

It's like the resurrection of
Isis came back to get
Her husband's sperm.

Uncivilized Wisdom.

R.O.N

R.O.N

GODDESS IMAGE

Egyptian Goddess,
African image.

A mirror reflection.
Heavenly sent from the
Earth.

A painted portrait filmed eternally.
A molded sculpture sent from the
Heavens placed here on
Earth.

A model, pure fashion.
Smell the sent of the ivory.
Made from the creation of a
Black Goddess of pure ebony.

The image of Cicely,
The beauty,
The smile of elegance.
The beat-up
Black image of our Mother.
The dark dirt roads as she walked barefoot,
Whipped wounds searching for
The end.
The creation of
A lady,
A woman.

Her image captured her beauty
Placed through filmography.

In the 30's graced us,
Blessed us in the 50's.

R.O.N

My Carmen Jones.
Sexy yet sensual in a
Red dress holding her own near
Belafonte'.

Our Marilyn Monroe,
A vocalist,
An actress from Cleveland to New York.

To the big screen.
To the cotton club,
To the Apollo,
To Halle Berry's portrayal of you.
The reincarnation of a
Queen.

The colorful image of
Betty Boop.

The legacy of
Baby Esther performing in a cabaret is missing.
The replacement of the
Black Goddess image is
Always hidden.

The legs on Josephine Baker.
The vocal tones of Lena.
Horns play melodically as we
Reminisce over
Aaliyah.

The high and exalted an immortal figure.

Queen of the Damned.
One in a million.
The caption of an
Earth tone picture another

R.O.N

Goddess like hidden figures.
Taraji, meaning hope
The head of an empire.
The hope
The pain
The life lessons.
The joys
The downs
The lows of
The suffering of anxiety and depression.

Where would we be without a
Woman's touch.
No longer my mammy
That label is gone with the wind.

The spirit of Hattie McDaniel
Is still with us.
As well as Coretta
Standing on a bright cloud by
Her King.

The image of an
Alluring creature,
Another piece of
A painting preprocessing. Your
Appearance is enchanting.

The stars are bright.
The natural beauty of Sanaa Lathan,
Regina King since her
Address was 227.
The sexiness and sense of humor of
Regina Hall.

The good deeds,
Thinking like a man.

R.O.N

The power of Being Mary Jane,
The mother, the wife,
The image of a Black barbie,
The smooth chocolate skin of
Gabrielle Union.

Dominican lady,
Mesmerized by your hips.
That body and attitude,
Lost for words.
My around the way girl
Your image isn't torn.

God was in an extra good mood
When he created you.

You even look good in that orange.
The new black image is self-contained.

Your image is complete.

The hard will and determination of
The Michelle Obama.
The intelligence of
The First Lady.

Keeping up with a Jones.
A dark complexion, image of grace.
Walking in the rain night clubbing.
Living my life, but a slave to
The rhythm a wild hurricane.

Portfolio with a
Bulletproof heart.
The price of fame.
A boomerang.

R.O.N

Shot a gem at a star,
As promised.
A United Kingdom, but
A mixture of Jamaican and Irish.
A constant struggle.

The Goddess image is defined.
The image?
Yes.

The Goddess image of
Angela Davis,
Kathleen Cleaver,
Assata Shakur combined.

Wisdom and intellect.

Protection and love even when
The storm is
The weather.
The writings and
The image is written on
The bronze wall.
The pen of Sonia Sanchez.
Maya Angelou,
The creative facet of
Ava DuVernay.

These images are put together.

Lena Waithe in this era of black beauty.
I see your images are great.

The black beauty of
Issa Rae, no insecurities.
The many completions
The floetic imagery of

· R.O.N

Amanda Seales.
From her comedy to a child,
A little young Queen in the 90's.

Chilling with my brother and me.

Goddess image,
Gazing into the eyes and listening to that
Sexy accent of Marsha Ambrosius,
As she recites her poetry.

No ordinary love captivating the
Sweet sounds of Sade.
My sweetest Taboo.
Sweet warming
Sauce.

Respect to a supreme image who gave birth to
Tracee Ellis Ross.

Goddess image, I honor you.

Even if I don't show it,
Goddess image.
That image was sent from
God.

R.O.N

R.O.N

PURPLE REIGN

Dear Lord,

I never thought I'd see this day.
The day me and my husband would be
Burying our little angel on
Her birthday.

Standing at these steps of the
Church people is
Crying,
Cannot understand this pain,
Cannot understand none of this.
Cannot understand this hurt of seeing your
Child in a
Casket.

I'm sick of the pain,
Sick and tired of the mass hysteria.
Sick of the unfortunate downfalls of our
Babies bleeding in
Black America.

How can I feel better?
I'm trying to stay warm in this
COLD ass weather.

My little princess
The pain will never vanish away.
My baby girl,
Little Nicky Baby aka **Reign**.

Me and your dad must honor you.

R.O.N

Your favorite roses are on
The side of your dad.
In the middle of the street, as he
Stares in shock.
Seated on his purple motorcycle.

Your favorite color.

I'm in the shadow in the back waiting for
The smoke to clear.
Up against the door,
Staring into the night, trying not to
Shed a tear.

Let me start from the beginning.
Let me start from the top.

Was home during quarantine,
When me and my angel
Decided to have some fun on
Tik Tok.

Hoping these hard times fly by.
Four days before
Reign would have turned five.
Bullets is flying right outside.
By the side of my home.

Normal activity.

These activities, I'm so sick of this.
Dancing to Beyonce,
When all of a sudden,
A bullet hit my little baby
In the chest.
Shock is an understatement.

R.O.N

Holding her little heart as she bled.
As I was attempting to cover
Reign, she was hit with one more to
Her head.

What type of world are we living in?
When you're not safe in your
Own home, with your own children.

They look at this as another
Black-on-Black blood war of a
Black-on-Black crime,
But hiding the fact that an
Innocent child was struck.

She was only four.

Where is the justice for baby reign?
Where are the politicians?
Where y'all at?
Where are these paid so-called activist?
Who claims lives matter, when
Your **BLACK**!

I don't see none of them, and
I'm wondering
Why??

Is it because my baby was a
Black child?

That in your eyes would eventually
Turn out a
Lost girl, that just so happens
To be **Black**., and
Who would eventually die.

R.O.N

Seems like we are just throwaways.
The **Black** child is crazy.
Savages in a dumpster next to
Brenda's baby.

Mommy and daddy will always love you,
My little

Purple Reign.

Baby I'm a star,
In your reflection in the clouds.
I'll try to sustain.
But my heart broke into two.

I pray every day,
Asking God to take me with you.
My only child, what has been done?
Seems like
God always takes the
Beautiful ones.

I am so hurt.
So sad, so angry. Cannot
Sleep easy without
Seeing my darling Nikki.
No justice, no peace,
I'm angry!
Let's go crazy in these streets.
Dreaming when doves cry,
Looking up at the sky
Looking at the staircase to heaven
We will finally meet.

The other day I was on
Social media,
Someone posted a

R.O.N

Picture of you and the caption was

"Justice for little **Reign**"

My heart turned warm, but
My computer blue.
Had to shut it off quick with all the
Sadness inside.
I would've took those bullets
I would die for you.

Until we meet again
Your spirit will remain
By my side.

Purple Reign.

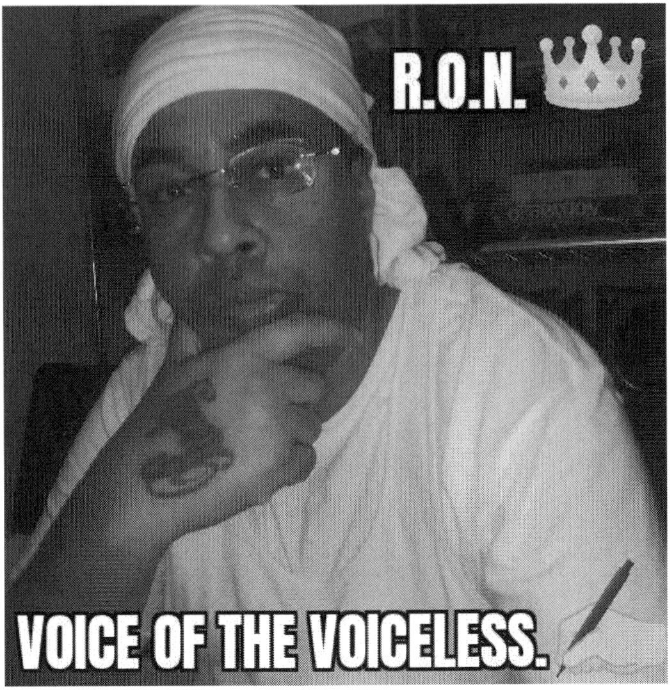
R.O.N.
VOICE OF THE VOICELESS.

ABOUT THE AUTHOR

Ron Caldwell is a poet/spoken word artist who writes from a unique perspective. Ron was born and raised in Rochester, New York.

From a very young age Ron has always had a vivid imagination. He always looked at life in a uniquely different and somewhat abnormal type of way. Since picking up a pen to painting pictures in a poetical art form at the tender young age of twelve.

Ron has a creative level that sets him apart from the rest. He writes about topics that may be viewed as dark, yet intriguing. He battled mental health issues and drug addiction and won.

Ron has always wanted to be the voice of the voiceless. He aspires to create a platform for his artistic expression and do something he always told his mother he would do.

Featured poems include Purple Reign, They Killed Cornbread, What Would Nip Do, & Dirty 30.

R.O.N

Made in the USA
Columbia, SC
18 August 2022